East African societies

Library of Man

Edited by Adam Kuper
Department of Anthropology,
University College London

Also in this series

Kenneth Little   *Urbanization as a Social Process*

A catalogue of social science books published by Routledge & Kegan Paul will be found at the end of this volume.

East African societies

Aylward Shorter

The Pastoral Institute of Eastern Africa
Gaba, Kampala

Routledge & Kegan Paul
London and Boston

First published in 1974
by Routledge & Kegan Paul Ltd
Broadway House, 68-74 Carter Lane,
London EC4V 5EL and
9 Park Street,
Boston, Mass. 02108, USA
Set in 10/12pt Times 327
and printed in Great Britain by
John Sherratt & Son Ltd, Park Road, Altrincham, Cheshire
WA14 5QQ

ISBN 0 7100 7957 5 (c)
ISBN 0 7100 7958 3 (p)
Library of Congress Catalog Card No. 74-81998

To Wandera Chagenda
and Young Africa's Lords of Language

Contents

		page
	Acknowledgments	ix
1	The anatomy of change in East Africa	1
2	Ecology and demography	10
3	Peopling theories and short history	18
4	Conservative pastoral societies	30
5	Chieftain societies	39
6	Urbanization	48
7	The rural revolution	57
8	Marriage and family life	66
9	Socialization and education	75
10	Religious trends	84
11	Spirit possession and communities of affliction	94
12	Witchcraft and sorcery	102
13	Case: The urban host tribe—the Ganda of Kampala	110
14	Case: The developing agricultural community—the Kamba of Kenya	118
15	Case: A rural re-settlement area in southern Tanzania	125
	Maps	133
	Notes	138
	Further reading	146
	Bibliography	147
	Index	150

Maps

		page
1	East Africa, Physical and Political	133
2	East Africa, Ethnic	134
3	Kampala City, Uganda	135
4	Ukambani, Kenya	136
5	Chunya Area, Tanzania	137

Acknowledgments

I am grateful to Dr Adam Kuper for his help in the planning of this book and for his useful suggestions during the early stages of writing it. I am also grateful to Professor Peter Rigby for information he kindly supplied about East African pastoral societies. I wish to thank Mr Njelu Kasaka for information he supplied about Tanzanian re-settlement areas, and the Rev. Peter Suttle for information about Ukambani. Finally, I am indebted to Mr Francis A. Lubowa for comments about the chapter on Kampala City.

The Pastoral Institute of Eastern Africa,
Gaba, Kampala

Aylward Shorter
July 1973

I

The anatomy of change in East Africa

An ethnography is a descriptive account of the culture and social institutions of a people. Such a description is doubly difficult in an area like East Africa. In the first place, East Africa is what is called a plural society, being culturally heterogeneous and fragmented. In the second place, it is subject at the present time to processes of rapid and widespread change. An ethnography of East Africa today necessarily entails generalization and comparison; it also demands some attempt to trace the diachronic processes of development and continuity and the ever more important processes of interaction and incorporation. In the past, social anthropologists were notoriously cautious about indulging in such activities, preferring instead to remain at the level of the seemingly homogeneous, self-sufficient and stable 'tribe'—or to use the modern euphemism 'ethnic group'. This preference for the microscopic has been highly productive. It has enabled the anthropologist to study whole structures and to penetrate deeply into systems of ideas. The microscopic interest has been further justified by the relative stability of small group relations in times of rapid social change. However, in the final analysis, the social anthropologists' reluctance to select a broader canvas has encouraged a false picture of East Africa, as a conglomeration of small societies that are static and discrete. Moreover, the illusion of stability that was created has made the phenomenon of social change more dramatic and incomprehensible than it really is.

The traditional form ethnography has taken in East Africa has been either the description of small, discrete, tribal entities, taken in isolation from each other, or else the large-scale survey or classification of such entities. A new generation of social anthropologists finds this approach altogether inadequate as a means of describing the various social processes in contemporary East Africa. Today the interest is in the mechanics of social change and the interaction between ethnic groups. The newer studies have challenged many of the assumptions on which the traditional ethnography was based. Chief among these assumptions were the following: that the tribe can be clearly discerned within precise limits; that ethnic groups can be classified according to a few criteria, or even one; that the so-called tribes were 'frozen' into clearly distinct groupings as a result of the colonial impact and that the most important consequence of decolonization and social change is a process of 'de-tribalization', according to which the tribes are disappearing. Added to these is the extreme view of Africans concerned to play down or reduce the embarrassment of tribalism, that the tribes were actually created by the colonial powers.

A tribe has been defined as a whole society, having a high degree of self-sufficiency at near-subsistence level, based on a relatively simple technology, without writing or literature (other than oral tradition), politically autonomous and with its own distinctive language, culture, sense of identity and religion.[1] Clearly such a definition no longer holds good today; and probably, even in pre-colonial times, was not absolutely verified. Tribal societies were not fully integral systems, although they possessed a higher degree of integration in the past than they do now. Probably, the fundamental reason for ethnic pluralism in East Africa was ecological adaptation combined with a relatively small population. This situation encouraged multiple adaptations and meant that a particular environment could support a variety of ethnic groups, each of which had made a different selection of the economic alternatives presented to it.

However, one must beware of over-emphasizing the factor of an identity of economic interests when discussing the foundations of ethnic loyalty. One must even avoid over-emphasizing the identity of political interests. Although it is true that ethnic groups were organized in the past as autonomous political units, a tribal loyalty can be fiercer today than in former times, and yet imply no commitment to the political structures of a primitive past. It has been well said that a tribe has 'an ideology of unity' rather than 'an identity of interests'.[2] Cultural factors such as language, ritual or other symbolism, or the sense of belonging to a historical, human tradition are, perhaps, more important. Such factors are certainly not subsidiary, and possess their own autonomy of motivation.

2

Even in pre-colonial times the tribe was in some sense a category of interaction. Tribal loyalties explained certain divisions, oppositions, alliances, and modes of behaviour between, and towards, different human groups. Today, the tribe is still a category of interaction, but it operates within a different, and much wider, system. Social change has given tribal loyalties a new importance and a new relevance. They can be invoked, for example, as a means of working out conflicts and tensions in the urban situation—as a vehicle for casting blame. They can be strengthened and enhanced by education and economic development. They can become even more important than kinship loyalties.

If tribal identities are somewhat blurred today, it is certainly true to say that their limits were by no means clear in former times. This is simply another way of saying that there were different points of reference for tribal loyalty, and that there was a measure of social—even structural—change. Tribal categories could be relative to an individual's geographical position, as in the well-known case of the categories Nyamwezi and Sukuma in Tanzania. Sukuma means 'northern', and the size of the category depends on how far north or south the speaker lives. Allegiance to sub-groups was also often of a relatively greater importance than allegiance to the more nebulous tribe. Even in chieftain societies, where great importance was attached to the territorial boundaries of chiefdoms, the frontiers between one ethnic group and another were far from clear, and chiefdoms aligned with different groupings in different situations.

Not only did regular, internal change occur in the traditional societies of East Africa in the pre-colonial period, but, at times, sweeping structural changes took place, as a result of conquests, dynastic migrations, and contact between peoples. Every tribal society had its non-conformists who were potential agents of social change. Nevertheless, it would be false to assert that the colonial powers of Britain and Germany 'froze' the tribes of East Africa into a state of immobility. Colonial government certainly placed a premium upon tribal loyalties, and tribal consciousness was heightened as a result. Arbitrary lists of tribes were compiled and administrators enlisted the aid of certain tribes with 'colonial' propensities, or emphasized the heterogeneity of groupings that were opposed to the colonial régime. But these activities encouraged rather than prevented the coming into existence of new ethnic groupings and the disappearance of others as a consequence of, or as a reaction to,

3

colonial administration. Such processes have continued even after the granting of independence and the formation of such 'super-tribes' or amalgams as the Abaluyia and the Kalenjin of Kenya are cases in point. The Germans and British did not 'create' tribes in any strict sense, but the colonial era, like the era of independence after it, did call for new forms of integration and did provide new areas of application for tribal loyalty.

Needless to say, 'detribalization' is a misleading term to apply to the phenomenon of social change in contemporary East Africa. Tribal allegiance is often of greater importance in urban areas and other situations created by modernization and the introduction of a sophisticated, western technology. East African towns have their component tribal villages, and tribal identity may be of equal importance in the multi-tribal, urban locations. Furthermore, urbanization is frequently characterized by the appearance of ethnic associations. One could as well speak of 'retribalization' as of 'detribalization' in many, if not most, instances, but the point is that those who use the term are referring to the problem of the adaptation of the individual to new social situations, rather than to change brought about in social institutions themselves. What is happening is that the individual, by social engineering and experimentation, is learning how to adapt and apply his ethnic loyalties to new experiences in a time of change. Urban life demands that many of the African townsman's traditional institutions and practices be modified, but many, also, are compatible with town life. Especially in the area of symbols, beliefs and values, tradition is tenacious. Moreover, co-existence is perfectly possible between different social systems and modes of life. There is much transience and mobility between urban and rural areas and the normal practice for the African who commutes between the two is to obey the conventions of the milieu in which he finds himself. This is not to say, of course, that the milieux do not influence each other as a result of this interaction, but it does show that pluralism is able to survive.

Obviously, if the tribe is hard to identify at any level, it is harder still to classify. Ethnic groups in East Africa cannot be classified unidimensionally, or according to a single criterion; they can be grouped in a number of different ways according to which factor, or factors, are selected. It might be thought that one is on surer ground when grouping the tribes on the basis of geography or history, yet even here there are pitfalls. Historical accidents have juxtaposed peoples of different cultures and origins, and have brought about far-reaching transformations in the cultures of tribes which share a common historical tradition. The ethnographer, today, must select factors which have validity for the contemporary social processes. Some of these factors may be historical, some geographical, some cultural, some ecological. Some factors affect certain ethnic groups more than others, but the idea of a comprehensive survey of East African tribes on the basis of a single set of factors can no longer be contemplated.

What, then, are the processes involved? East Africa is experiencing structural and organizational change. Not only are the structures of society being radically altered, but the scale of relationships is being enlarged. There is a greater intensity, and a greater extensiveness, of co-operation and communication between the various units of East African society. This is not only a matter of geographical distance, of postal systems, telephone, migrant labour, the holding of meetings and so on. It is also a question of specialization, through which a particular unit of society can serve the others and the different units become functionally interdependent. It is also a question of a growth of common identity, and in this connection one is tempted to think first of all of the process of nation building. However, the nation is not the only, nor the most influential, focus for a congruence of values. Many forms of common identity are arising, which are at once larger than the tribe and smaller than the nation, and which overlap one another. One thinks, in particular, of religious affiliations, and of bonds created by modern education in its different forms, and at its different levels. Some forms of common identity overlap the frontiers of the nation or transcend the nation altogether. Such may be the common adherence to values bequeathed by the colonial power, to regional, or to pan-African ideals. In the case of a plural society, the term 'national culture' has little meaning. There is, of course, no homogeneous culture; and at best only a small area of congruence of values. If in Britain, for example, 'British culture' is taken to include Scottish dancing, Welsh community singing, and West Country folk songs, then it is even more likely that national culture in the East African countries will be similarly heterogeneous. A developing national culture means, in fact, a developing knowledge by the ethnic groups of each other's cultural heritage, and a developing appreciation of it.

The process of absorption that results from the interaction of

5

different ethnic groups and social units is known as incorporation.[3] Even in those countries where complete incorporation is assumed to be the ideal, it is rarely, if ever, achieved. Likewise, the total absence of incorporation is impossible. Incorporation is a matter of degree, and one can only say that some nations achieve a higher degree of incorporation than others. The difficulty is that incorporation is not an even process, following a single line of evolution. On the contrary, it takes place against a background of continual shifts and variations, of migrations, of stratification, in which each unit is continually adjusting to other units and to the whole. This means that the degree of cohesion varies at different moments, and that units take on different degrees of importance with respect to each other. Change, today, is not only more widespread, it is also more rapid. Cultures or sub-cultures come into existence more easily, often between generations, as for example, recognizable youth cultures. This means that the periods of stability between the movement of change are reduced to a minimum. The consequence of all this is that individuals have to live out their lives in an extremely complex situation. As Professor Southall, a well-known student of East African society, has written: 'To hammer home the importance of interlocking, overlapping, multiple and alternative, collective entities is one of the most important messages of social and cultural anthropology'.[4]

Pluralism is a growing phenomenon in the world at large and, to some extent, East Africa is sharing in this world experience through her contacts with western and other countries, and especially through her acceptance of a technology developed outside Africa, a technology which serves a variety of cultures and value systems different from her own. Nevertheless, East Africa brings her own traditional, cultural and structural complexity to meet the influences which bear upon her from outside. Africans are selective in their approach to elements of foreign culture. They approve some and reject others. Moreover, they are capable of giving them an altogether new meaning and function. In the long run, deep-seated value-systems, based as they are upon a fundamentally religious view of man and the world, prove to be remarkably resilient in the modern situation, in spite of the adoption of new techniques and new forms of social organization. Human traditions are strong. This means that social change in modern East Africa is not a heraclitean process which is completely unintelligible to the observer. Elements of continuity exist and patterns can be discerned. It is for the ethnographer to note and record them.

Not all the processes are positive or contributory to incorporation. Tribalism is the term usually applied to an imbalance of privileges, opportunities and profits among the tribes and it is a major cause of disunity and opposition in modern East Africa. In most multi-tribal situations, it still pays, as it is said, 'to do one's tribal arithmetic'. On the other hand, the modernizing process may give different tribes varied vocations and goals in relation to the wider, national entity. Many political leaders derive their power from a strong tribal base, in which case the tribe is deemed to have a national vocation. The Kikuyu of Kenya are, perhaps, a case in point. Other leaders have been able to build up their power on a multi-tribal base, and some have been able to build up nationalist movements on a variety of non-tribal centres. In general, all the East African governments have favoured one-party states, believing—with justification—that multi-party systems favour tribalism.

Besides tribalism, there is what Professor Gulliver has called 'particularism' and this usually takes the form of a commitment to an old style of life.[5] Particularism is a reluctance—even a refusal—to change, and it typifies the highly specialized ethnic groups, notably the pastoralist tribes. In a later chapter there is a discussion about the conservative commitment of cattle-raising people in East Africa. Here it need only be said that, granted the validity of their particular economic specialization, modernization and change offers such people very little real advantage. On the contrary, social change and technological development appears to militate against them, and they take up an extreme, defensive attitude.

East Africa's pluralism was traditionally a political, as well as a cultural, pluralism, as we have seen. The fact, however, that the ethnic groups were deprived of their political power does not mean that political pluralism has ceased to exist. On the contrary, the colonial period was characterized by a structural pluralism in which minority racial segments, European and Asian, controlled the political and economic power. This type of pluralism tends to persist, even after the departure of Europeans and Asians, with the perpetuation of small, ruling and entrepreneurial classes.

In the other chapters that follow, the changing shape of East African society will be examined in the light of certain prominent factors. One of these is the very obvious example of social change, urbanization. Urbanization has been strikingly rapid in East Africa, but it still directly affects only a very small percentage of the population. Indeed, it has been argued that the most wide-ranging revolution is taking place in the rural areas, and not in the towns. In spite of a relative discontinuity between town and country, a modernization is taking place that is sometimes referred to as 'urbanism', 'anticipatory urbanization' or the spread of 'an urban mentality'. Without denying the influence of the towns as centres of communication and political dominance, it is possible that such terms tend to exaggerate the extent of urban influence. What is happening, in any case, is that structural change is taking place, markets are being brought into being, new roles are being created, and the position of women, for example, is being altered. Such change affects the traditional structures of kinship and family life, let alone the traditional social and political structures.

Another line of enquiry is that of the evolution or demise of the traditional ruler, and here in particular there has to be a discussion of the chieftain societies which, in East Africa, are widely linked by historical movements and traditions and whose institutions are central to a very large number of cultures. Religion, also, is a highly important factor. Although religious beliefs and ideas often had a currency wider than within a given tribe, the practice of religion and its inculcation in succeeding generations depended to a great extent on the social structure of the tribe. These structures are changing or breaking up, and the old expressive community rituals that inculcated the beliefs are either disappearing or shrinking to become merely family celebrations. The question has to be asked: to what extent are the so-called immigrant religions of Christianity and Islam, and the unsophisticated syntheses represented by the independent churches able to articulate and develop the values of traditional religion and give East Africans a framework for understanding their present life in a rapidly changing society?

If religious rituals are threatened, the so-called instrumental rituals of power are apparently flourishing and discovering new areas of application. Divination and witchcraft accusation are very common forms in which tensions and oppositions are worked out in a highly competitive, modern society. Spirit possession, also, and what Professor Turner has called 'communities of affliction' also have their importance in East Africa, often symbolizing, in their preoccupation with bodily ills, the ills that beset an ailing social order, and the desire to rebuild a strong and clearly discernible society. It may be that people in East Africa will be cheated of this hope, and that the society of the future will be less clearly delineated and less stable than the tribal societies of the past. A short ethnography of this kind can only point out the trends, and attempt to understand some of their social causes and consequences.

2

Ecology and demography

Underlying the social and cultural complexity of East Africa is the complexity of the physical environment.[1] East Africa enjoys a considerable variety of climate, terrain and vegetation. Basically, the greater part of the area is a vast, crystalline plateau, rising from a narrow coastal belt to a general altitude of between 3,000 and 6,000 feet above sea-level. This plateau is cleft by an immense series of valleys, known collectively as the Great Rift Valley, a gigantic crack appearing in the surface of the earth at the time of its formation. Within and between the Rift lie the great lakes of East Africa, the largest of them being Lakes Victoria, Tanganyika, Malawi (Nyasa), Rudolf, Albert, Kyoga, George, Edward and Rukwa. The depth of the lakes varies considerably. Tanganyika and Malawi are extremely deep, while Victoria is relatively shallow, and Lake Rukwa is subject to so much evaporation that it has been known to disappear entirely. Two of the great rivers of Africa rise from the East African Lakes, the Nile which takes its origin from Lakes Victoria and Albert, and the Congo which is partially fed by Lake Tanganyika and Lake Mweru. For the rest, there are relatively few rivers, the Rufiji and Pangani in Tanzania and the Tana in Kenya being the most important.

Rising from the East African plateau are a number of highland areas, some of them crowned by high, snow-capped mountains or mountain ranges. Mount Kilimanjaro in Tanzania, at 19,340 feet, is the highest African mountain, and the highest single mountain in the world. Its sister Mount Kenya rises to 17,058 feet and, like Mount Kilimanjaro, is an ancient volcano. Other high mountains are the Ruwenzori Range at 16,794 feet and Mount Elgon at 14,176 feet, both in Uganda.

10

There are four main types of vegetation in East Africa. The first is the tropical forest-savanna of the coastal belt, a sedimentary plain with river outlets and lagoons. The second type is found mainly in the north-east of the region, a somewhat dry area of grass, bushland and thicket. In northern Kenya this even becomes a desert or semi-desert, but all three East African countries have their share of bush-land. The third main type of vegetation is the usually moist wood-land-savanna known locally as *miombo* and mainly composed of trees of the *brachystegia* species. Finally, there are the forest regions, both the high altitude forests on the mountain slopes, and the equat-orial rain forests found mainly in western Uganda.

The equator crosses the northern half of the region, through Kenya and Uganda, but the altitude ensures a reasonably mild climate. Over most of East Africa the temperature averages between 20 and 30°C. From October to April most areas have rain, the heavi-est rainfall being at the coast, in the lake areas and in the highlands. During the rest of the year large areas of northern Kenya and central and southern Tanzania have no rain at all. The coastal, highland and lake-shore regions, however, continue to enjoy a monthly rainfall of from 5 to 15 cm (2 to 6″).

Basically, the fertile areas of high rainfall can be reduced to six: the Kenya coast, the central highlands of Kenya, the northern shores of Lake Victoria in Kenya, Uganda and Tanzania, the highlands round Mount Kilimanjaro, the Kigezi highlands of south-western Uganda and the southern highlands of Tanzania on the northern tip of Lake Malawi (Nyasa). In these places bananas are grown and in most cases form the staple diet. These are the areas which support the densest populations. Millet, sorghum and maize are grown for food elsewhere, while rice is grown mainly at the coast and on the southern shores of Lake Victoria. Coconut palms are mainly found only along the coast but groundnuts are grown almost everywhere and cassava is found in a great many places as a standby in time of famine.

In Uganda the cash crops coffee and cotton are the mainstays of the economy, but in recent years the output of tea, tobacco and sugar has slowly risen. Kenya has considerably more diversification of its agricultural products: coffee, tea, maize, sisal, wheat, pyre-thrum and sugar. Tanzania, however, has an excessive dependence on pyrethrum and sisal, of which it is the world's largest producer. The coral rock islands of Zanzibar and Pemba which belong to the

Tanzanian Republic are responsible for more than a third of the world's annual production of cloves, but Tanzania as a whole has other, lesser cash crops: coffee, sugar, cotton, tea and tobacco. In Uganda and Kenya much of the farming is organized by large companies and corporations, although about 50 per cent of the production is in the hands of small-holders. In Tanzania, state farms still play an important part, but recently, according to the country's socialist ideology, block farms known as '*ujamaa* villages' have been begun in many places. In 1971 nearly a million people moved to these new villages. In spite of the increase of cash crops, farming is still, in many areas, a matter of subsistence only. The universal implement is the hoe, although in places where cattle are raised, the ox-plough is also in use. Agricultural machinery has been introduced into the larger plantations and the block farms.

Cattle-raising has depended on the extent to which the country is free of infestation by the tsetse fly, a blood-sucking insect which transmits the trypanosome parasite to animals. The favourite habitat of the fly is *miombo* woodland, the type of vegetation which covers about 50 per cent of East Africa. This means that although wild animals which are tolerant of the parasite can live in these areas, domestic animals such as sheep, goats, pigs, and especially cattle are confined to areas which are free of fly. In practice such areas are: south-western and central Kenya; central, eastern, and south-western Uganda; a central corridor in Tanzania, and the areas immediately south of Lake Victoria and north of Lake Malawi. Dairy farming has considerable importance in Kenya, and Uganda is approaching self-sufficiency in dairy produce. Tanzania, in which most of the tsetse infestation is found, is less fortunate.

Miombo woodland, however, has its uses. This is the vegetation which characterizes the national parks with their abundant herds of antelope, their elephants, hippopotami, rhinoceros, giraffes, lions, leopards, wild pigs, wart-hogs and magnificent bird life. Although continual inroads are made by African poachers, and although maintaining the balance between the animal populations becomes daily more difficult, East Africa still boasts game and bird sanctuaries which are among the most spectacular in the world. In all three East African countries tourism is now a booming industry, but even the influx of tourists can constitute a danger to certain species of animal. This is especially the case of the crocodiles on the Victoria Nile whose breeding grounds are disturbed by boat loads of tourists.

12

Miombo woodland is sparsely inhabited, usually by shifting grain cultivators, employing slash-and-burn techniques, and practising hunting and gathering. In many places honey-collecting is a characteristic activity. This entails either robbing the nests of the honey bee in the trees, or hanging a barrage of bark hives to trap some of the numerous swarms in the early dry season. Honey and wax production have assumed some importance in areas where co-operatives have been set up, and bee products are even exported. Fishing supplements the diet of a great many East African communities but at the coast, along the major rivers and on the lake shores it has become an important industry, supplying fresh and dried fish to inland communities.

Although minerals are present in East Africa in varying quantities, it cannot be said that there are any great mining prospects.[2] Uganda has seen a recent rise in copper mining and the mining of some other minerals, while Tanzania continues to operate the diamond mine at Mwadui, and to exploit small quantities of gold, salt, tin, mica, silver, gypsum and magnetite. The 1930s saw a minor gold-rush on the Lupa River and its tributaries, but the workings were almost exhausted when the Second World War broke out and administered the *coup de grâce*. Kenya is not a mining country, but has small deposits of copper, magnesium, salt, asbestos and gold. More important, perhaps, are the natural deposits of soda.

All three East African countries now have hydro-electric power supplies. In Uganda the very source of the Nile at Owen Falls, Jinja, has been harnessed and has the biggest output, some 165,000 kilowatts per annum. The Tana River scheme in Kenya and the Nyumba-ya-Mungu dam at Moshi in Tanzania are less powerful, and Kenya has been taking a good deal of its power supply from Uganda up to now. Manufacturing is not a significant aspect of the economy of any of these countries, but there has been considerable expansion. Kenya is economically the most advanced of the three countries and has the most numerous and varied manufacturing industries. However, both Uganda and Tanzania have their breweries, textile factories, meat packers, sugar refiners, soap manufacturers and cement and steel works. The processing of agricultural and dairy products are important in all the countries: coffee and sugar refining, tea processing, cotton ginning, oil milling, dairies, and so on.

Tourism is playing an ever-increasing part in the economy of East Africa. The biggest beneficiary is Kenya, where the numbers of tourists have been increasing annually by 20 per cent over the past few years. It is reckoned that by 1975, 500,000 tourists will come to Kenya each year and earn the country £52 million. Uganda and Tanzania have not been so lucky, partly because Kenya is better organized and more accessible, and partly because the other countries are in need of a better image abroad. Uganda has lacked political stability and harmony between her different ethnic groups. Tanzania has earned the reputation of being a radically socialist country, receiving massive aid from communist countries, and, at least initially, hostile to western tourists.

It was obvious from very early days that mutual benefit would accrue to all the East African countries if there were a pooling of administrative resources. As early as 1947 an East Africa High Commission was set up, with a Legislative Assembly meeting in turn in each of the three capitals, Nairobi, Kampala and Dar-es-Salaam. At independence this High Commission became the Common Services Organization, known later as the East African Common Market or East African Community. Common authorities were set up to deal with services such as taxation, customs and excise, railways, harbours, posts, telegraphs and airways. The East African Community continues to function, even though it has undergone considerable strain both from the economic inequalities of the partners and from disparities arising from their different political ideologies. Kenya's pro-western tendencies encourage a greater measure of western investment. If the East African Community is to survive, Kenya has to allow Tanzania and Uganda to grow, even at the expense of her own immediate interests. Tanzania is pursuing a socialist policy which demands low salary scales. This is bound to invite unfavourable comparison with the scales of Community employees from Uganda and Kenya. Also affecting the working of the Community are the stringent currency regulations made by each of the countries, particularly by Uganda and Tanzania, to protect their foreign reserves.

Of the three countries, Tanzania has the largest surface area, 363,708 square miles, and the largest population, approaching 13 million.[3] However, its population is the least dense, at 34 per square mile. Uganda has the smallest land area, 93,981 square miles, and the smallest population, 9,800,000, but its density is the highest of the three countries, 90 per square mile. Kenya has a total population approaching 11 million, living in a land area of 224,960 square miles and its density is 40 per square mile. Kenya has the highest growth rate of population, 3·3 per cent per annum, while Tanzania and Uganda have a current growth rate of 2·9 per cent and 2·7 per cent, respectively. More will be said, in a later chapter, on urban growth in East Africa, but the three countries are very little urbanized. Kenya, with the population of its capital city, Nairobi, standing at half a million and an urban population which represents 16 per cent of the total, is the most urbanized.

In Kenya the largest ethnic group, the Kikuyu, count nearly two million people, and is the 'host tribe' of the capital, Nairobi. The next largest ethnic group is that of the Luo who count just over a million. The Luo differ widely in language and culture from the Kikuyu and are their most serious political rivals. They are the host tribe for the important town and port of Kisumu on Lake Victoria. Finally, in the third place, comes the 'super-tribe' of the Luyia, an amalgam of a dozen or so smaller groups with a growing sense of common identity. The Luyia just top the million mark. Kenya has a population of some 140,000 Asians, a minority of whom are Kenyan citizens. The rest are citizens of Britain, India, Pakistan or Bangladesh. Most of them are either traders, businessmen, technicians, teachers or professional people. At the beginning of the century, rigid racial and social barriers cut the Asians off from other sections of the population. Over the years a new generation has arisen, influenced by a western system of education, higher standards of living and fluency in English. This has made for a greater measure of integration, particularly in the Ismaeli (Muslim) and Goan communities. However, since political independence, they have become more vulnerable and the pressures of Africanization and the demands for a redistribution of wealth have led to a growing criticism of their socio-economic position. All three East African countries have an immigrant community of Asians.

Kenya also has a community of 40,000 Arabs, mostly living at the coast, in and around the town and port of Mombasa which counts a total population of a quarter of a million. The Arabs, as we shall see, have a longer history in Kenya than the Asians. Finally, among the immigrant communities of Kenya are some 43,000 Europeans. Of these, a minority have settled in Kenya, but most are probably present on a short-term basis as missionaries, teachers, technicians, businessmen and professional people. The largest group among them are British.

In Uganda far and away the largest ethnic group is that of the Ganda, the host tribe of the capital city, Kampala. The Ganda number nearly two million, about one-fifth of the total population of the country. Of the immigrant communities, in August 1972 it was reckoned that the Asians numbered about 80,000, 36,500 of them being British subjects. Of the remainder, a minority was Ugandan. At the end of 1972 all non-Ugandan Asians were expelled by the government, except for a small number of technicians, teachers and professionals whose presence was vitally necessary. By mid-1973 there were only about 2,000 Asians of all nationalities remaining in the country. In 1969 there were some 11,000 Europeans in Uganda, 6,000 of them British. In 1973 the latter numbered only about 2,000, and other European nationalities had also dwindled, most of them being in the country on a short-term basis.

In Tanzania, the ethnic groups are more numerous and there is less numerical disparity between them. The largest ethnic groups are the Sukuma and Nyamwezi, usually listed separately, although the distinction between them is largely academic. The Sukuma count more than half a million, while the Nyamwezi are probably now near a quarter of a million. The other principal groups are the Ha, Makonde, Gogo, Haya, Chagga, Hehe and Zulu. There are 26,000 Arabs, the majority probably living at the coast, although Arab small traders are also found scattered inland. The host tribe of the coastal capital, Dar-es-Salaam, is the relatively insignificant Zaramo group and the recent growth of the city suggests that they will be outnumbered by people of other groups before very long. Asians in Tanzania number about 85,000—as elsewhere in Africa, they are citizens of Britain, India, Pakistan and Bangladesh, as well as of their country of residence. Considerable social and economic pressure has reduced their number in Tanzania, but there have been no forced expulsions as in Uganda. Europeans number 15,000, a tiny fraction of whom have settled in the country.

The population growth rates in all three countries are in advance of the growth rate of the world's population as a whole. A rise in the birth rate, coupled with increased chances of survival for infants and children, has brought about a situation in which an extremely large proportion of the total population of East Africa consists of children and adolescents. In Tanzania and Uganda, for example, more than half the population (54 per cent) is under the age of twenty. This fact will, no doubt, lead to ever more over-crowding in the fertile and densely populated areas, and it will also create immense social problems. It is still too early to decide whether a predominantly young population will make for a greater degree of incorporation, or will increase the problem of disorientation. Whichever happens, it is likely to contribute to the pace and the extent of change.

To sum up this chapter, therefore, East African development must be mainly agricultural development, but it is hampered by factors such as soil fertility, lack of water and rain, and the presence of the tsetse fly. At present such problems are too large to be completely overcome. This means that clearly defined areas exist in East Africa, within which there is a limited range of particular economic choices, and this fact accounts for the major differences of patterns of movement and settlement between the different ethnic groups. It also accounts for the extremes of population density and sparseness that are found in the region. In this way diversity of environment clearly contributes to the basic pluralism of East Africa.

3

Peopling theories and short history

The reconstruction of East Africa's remote past is bedevilled by three initial problems—the ever-present factor of complexity, the factor of conscious or unconscious prejudice among writers and scholars, and the confusion of terminology. It has already been noted that East Africa is culturally, linguistically and racially heterogeneous. One cannot, as some writers have done, assume an easy equation between culture, language and physical characteristics. On the contrary, there is much overlapping. In the evolution of East African peoples as we know them today, different layers have overlaid each other, and there have been varying degrees of mutual influence between different traditions. Moreover, some languages and cultures which have played an important part in the evolutionary process have become submerged, or have vanished altogether.

Both European and African writers alike have displayed prejudice in their handling and interpretation of material. Early European scholars like Seligman, for example, assumed that Europe and the Near East were points of diffusion of culture, language and race in Africa.[1] They explained the peopling of Africa in terms of successive waves of invasion from the north-east. Races like those in north-east Africa which are intermediate between the African Negro and the European Caucasian were claimed as belonging to the 'European' sphere and their remarkable civilizations as belonging to the history of western civilization. Terms such as 'the brown race' or 'Hamite' were used and the cultural achievements of Negro peoples were attributed to this 'superior race'. Recent decades have witnessed the gradual dismantling of the 'Hamitic myth' and some African writers, Anta Diop, for example, have even gone so far as to claim the brown race as Negroes and their civilizations as an apanage of

18

Negro Africa.[2] This is really the Hamitic myth in reverse. The truth, however, according to Oscar Wilde's epigram, 'is seldom pure and never simple', and some attempt must be made in this chapter to disentangle it. In one respect, however, early writers were probably correct. East Africa is a crucial area and the complexity and variety of its peoples and cultures is relevant for Africa as a whole.

In the early theories, the terminologies of physical anthropology, cultural anthropology and linguistics have been confused. Strictly speaking, Hamitic is a linguistic category, as is Bantu. On the other hand, Negro is a physical, or racial term, and Bushman-Hottentot refers rather to a specific culture. Seligman and Baumann took racial characteristics as their starting point, and attempted to identify the 'original' or 'pure' races. Having done this, they hoped to show how the modern situation was the result of racial mixtures. Language and culture were assumed to be concomitants of race. Seligman proposed three 'pure' races: the Hamite, the Bushman and the Negro. According to his theory, the original inhabitants of East Africa were Bushmen (sometimes called Khoisan), and they were followed by successive waves of Hamites and Negroes. The mixture of Negro and Hamite in which Negro predominated produced the Bantu, and the mixture of Negro and Hamite in which the Hamite predominated produced the Nilote (from the Nile Valley region). Finally, the mixture of the Nilote and the Hamite produced the Nilo-Hamite or Half-Hamite, the term given to a number of pastoral or semi-pastoral peoples in East Africa.

Baumann, on the other hand, held that there were four original races for Africa as a whole: Pygmies, Bushman-Hottentot, Eurasian and Negro.[3] The Ethiopeans were a mixture of Eurasian and Negro; the Bantu a mixture of Negro, Ethiopian and Bushman-Hottentot, and the Nilotes a mixture of Negro and Ethiopian without the Bushman element. Other mixtures included the Virgin Forest Negroes who were deemed to be composed of Pygmy and Bantu; and also the North Africans, a mixture of Eurasian and Ethiopian.

Needless to say, much of this theorizing was pure conjecture. Physical anthropologists today are hesitant about plotting the influence which one population has on the physical make-up of another. The measurement of so-called multi-variate distances is based on the degree of similarity between two groups of people for a set of biological variables (such as blood groups, body measurements, etc.) computed as a general 'distance' between them. Such measurement offers support for evidence of other kinds, linguistic, cultural, historical. It can hardly stand on its own, nor can it be made a starting point for a theory of how East Africa was peopled. In the case of the Bantu, as we shall see, multi-variate distances indicate that a certain physical type does, in fact, correspond to a particular language group. In general, physical anthropologists or anthropo-biologists content themselves with descriptive classifications. Trevor's morphological classification, for example, includes the three main categories, Caucasiform, Negriform and Khoisaniform.[4] His Negriform category includes the Negrillo or Pygmy group, as well as the various types of Negro, Sudanian, Guinean, Congolian, Nilote and Zingian.

Whatever influence the different races have had on each other, it is clear that allowance must be made for evolution as a result of selective forces, operating in particular physical environments. The pastoralists in the dry belt on the northern and eastern fringes of sub-Saharan Africa evolved a peculiar physique adapted to conditions of extreme heat—tall and spare, with relatively little body weight. The small stature of the Pygmy owes a great deal to his forest environment, while even the differentiation of the Negro himself is attributable to conditions prevailing on the forest fringe.

As the paleontological discoveries at Olduvai gorge have shown, East Africa was the centre of the inhabited world at the very dawn of human history. It is not easy, however, to work out the precise relationship of the varieties of homo sapiens who have inhabited the area in historical times, to those early tool-makers whose remains have been discovered by Dr Leakey and his associates. It seems probable that a dominant type eventually emerged, possessing the physical characteristics of the Bushman, short and slight of build, steatopygous and with a yellow-brown skin colour.[5] The Hadza hunters of Lake Eyasi and the Sandawe of central Tanzania would be the remnants of this early population. They were probably already widely distributed over East Africa before 1000 B.C. It is not clear whether the Pygmies are derived from Negro or from Bushman stock. There are Pygmies today in Uganda, living along the Zaïre border, and there is little doubt that they were more widely spread at one time. Whether they were related to the Bushman settlers of East Africa, or whether they were an off-shoot of the already flourishing Negro population in Western Africa, it is likely that they inhabited the relatively restricted forest regions at the same period.

Around 1000 B.C. a people of mixed Caucasian and Negro race came south into East Africa from Ethiopia. They spoke a Cushitic language, from a sub-group of the Hamitico-Semitic family of languages, modern examples of which are Galla, Somali and Sidama. These people were cattle herders and sheep rearers, and they occupied the grassland corridor, stretching from Kenya into northern Tanzania. There are still small pockets of Cushitic speakers in East Africa, for example the Galla of northern Kenya and the Iraqw or Mbulu of Tanzania.

Then in about A.D. 1000 came the Negro peoples, speakers of Bantu languages, filtering into East Africa in small groups from the south and west. A hundred years ago Bleek coined the name Bantu for peoples speaking languages with certain obvious similarities, in particular, noun classes distinguished by prefixes. A word common—though in a variety of forms—to many of these languages was *umuntu*, man, *abantu*, men. Hence Bantu. Linguists today, however, are not content with superficial comparisons. Their studies of the grammatical structures of these languages and their lexical units or word-roots reveal a complex situation. In particular, controversy has centred on Bantu origins. Guthrie listed some 2,300 word roots in 200 Bantu languages.[6] He discovered that 500 of these roots were distributed throughout the whole area in which Bantu languages are spoken, each root occurring in at least two of twelve Bantu zones. He then plotted the percentage of these common Bantu roots retained by each language and discovered that there existed a central, nuclear area which retained 43 per cent and more. This area forms an ellipse, stretching from the mouth of the Congo or Zaïre River in the west, to the mouth of the Rovuma River on the east coast of Tanzania. Thus the Bantu Ellipse, as it has been called, stretches across the southern part of East Africa. Guthrie has argued that it is this central, nuclear region which forms the point of origin of the Bantu-speaking peoples.

Greenberg disagrees with Guthrie, arguing that the area of the greatest conservatism is not necessarily the area of origin.[7] If this were the case, then Germanic languages would have to originate in Iceland where the greatest number of Germanic roots are retained. On a similar showing, the Romance languages would originate in Sardinia, and Great Britain with its highly developed dialects could be challenged as the point of origin for the English spoken more uniformly in other parts of the world. Greenberg believes that the

21

north-western Bantu area is older, in spite of its greater variation. On the basis of a study of 400 items, viewed both lexically and grammatically, in a large number of African languages, he places Bantu as a sub-group within the Niger-Congo family of languages, with its point of origin in the middle Benue area of Nigeria.

Greenberg's hypothesis is not an absolute contradiction of Guthrie's. On the contrary, it can be plausibly maintained that, while the ultimate point of origin for the Bantu languages lies in the north-west of the continent, there was a subsequent differentiation in the central, elliptical area and that this accounts for the differences between the western and eastern Bantu. One thing, however, is clear, whichever theory is held: Bantu, as a new family of languages, expanded very rapidly indeed in order to achieve such a wide geographical dispersion with such a small degree of divergence.

In any case, we can be sure that, in East Africa, it is with the eastern Bantu that we have to deal. Moreover, archaeological evidence for pottery types appears to confirm the hypothesis of the Bantu spreading from the south and west, bringing with them a knowledge of iron-working and farming.[8] It also confirms the picture of a rapid expansion. The anthropobiological evidence of multivariate distances. already referred to, confirms the idea of the Bantu Ellipse, since it shows that there is a relative physical homogeneity in the same area. The Bantu speakers probably entered East Africa through the corridors that lie between Lakes Tanganyika, Mweru, Bangweolo, and Malawi (Nyasa). They may have also filtered through the corridor between Lake Kivu and Lake Tanganyika. They occupied the highland areas and areas of high rainfall first of all. Here they cultivated the banana as the staple and developed dense populations. Later on they began to disperse from these highland areas, sending small groups down into the less fertile plains and valleys to compete with, or to transform, the surviving Bushmen, practising a mixture of hunting, gathering and shifting grain cultivation.

After A.D. 1000 groups of Negro peoples, speaking eastern Sudanic or Nilotic languages, moved south from the Nile area in present day Sudan. One group came down to the Kenya highlands and northern Tanzania and assimilated the Cushitic speakers they found there. Their language, although mixed in origin, had a Cushitic emphasis. Today they are represented by the Kalenjin peoples of the western Kenya Highlands and by the Taturu or Tatoga (also called Mangati) of Tanzania. Another group moved down the grassland corridor of Kenya and northern Tanzania, absorbing some of the highland group and ousting the others. They were pastoralists and their modern representatives are the Masai and other related peoples.

A final group moved down the Nile in the sixteenth century to modern Uganda, and thence into Kenya and Tanzania around the eastern shores of Lake Victoria. These were the Lwoo speakers who had little Cushitic influence, and some of the second group were influenced by them to the extent of adopting their language. They appear to have exerted pressure on the Bantu, bringing to an end the ascendancy of the kingdom of Bunyoro-Kitara. The Bantu, however, clung to their highland areas and, especially through the development of the Kingdom of Buganda, succeeded in restoring their influence. The Uganda or central Lwoo are represented by the Alur, the Chope and the Acholi; the eastern Lwoo, on the Kenya-Uganda border, and on the western shores of Lake Victoria in Kenya and Tanzania, by the Padhola and the Luo.

Among the Bantu there were apparently few clearly defined migrations. Their descent into the lowland areas probably involved small dynastic groups. However, according to oral tradition, there were a number of discernible points of dispersal. One of these was the area of the Taita hills in south-eastern Kenya, near Mount Kilimanjaro, from which several peoples in eastern Kenya and north-eastern Tanzania take their origin. In Kenya the groups moved north-east to the legendary Shungwaya, between the Tana and Juba rivers. This in turn became a second dispersal area, whence they move southwards, down the coast. The Lake Kingdom area of Uganda was another point of dispersal, from which people moved eastwards and southwards, along the western shores of Lake Victoria. Oral traditions link a great many peoples in western Tanzania with the northern Lake area, in particular the traditions of the legendary Chwezi or Swezi which undergo a variety of transpositions and transformations.[9] The Lake Corridor between Lakes Malawi (Nyasa) and Tanganyika was another area of movement and dispersal, for the people of the southern highlands. Yet another highland dispersal area was that of the Pare Mountains in north-eastern Tanzania, a point of origin for a number of peoples in southern Kenya and northern Tanzania. Finally, the Nguru and Luguru mountains of eastern Tanzania, known to the peoples of the west by the loose designation of Usagara, were a dispersal area for groups moving westwards into the interior. It is probable that the stimulus provided by this movement was an important factor in drawing the Nyamwezi peoples to the coast, and in developing long distance porterage.

Apart from the movement of the Nilotic peoples, already described, there were at least three other migrations, properly so-called. At the end of the sixteenth century a ferocious people called the Zimba moved up the coast from Mozambique into modern Kenya, attacking the coastal towns one after the other, and disappearing as mysteriously as they came.[10] In the mid-eighteenth century, the Tusi people from Rwanda-Burundi moved south into Ufipa in south-western Tanzania and founded dynasties there. They continued exerting pressure on west-central Tanzania until about 1840. Lastly, came the Ngoni in their great migration northwards from South Africa. They crossed the Zambezi River in 1835 and came up into Tanzania in two columns, one on either side of Lake Malawi (Nyasa). The western column finally reached Lake Victoria in the 1850s.

The East African coast was known to navigators in Graeco-Roman times, and the navigation guide composed by a Greek merchant seaman in about A.D. 80 has come down to us.[11] This is known as the *Periplus of the Erythrean Sea* and describes a flourishing trade in ivory and slaves, conducted by Arabs. Arab books reveal that, from the sixth to the sixteenth century, East Africa had an important place in a wide network of trade all over the Indian Ocean, a trade over which the Arabs were the undisputed masters. The Arabs came, for the most part, from the district of Oman in south-eastern Arabia, and by the eleventh century there was a chain of Arab coastal colonies running from Mogadishu to Sofala. Portuguese explorers reached the East African coast at the end of the fifteenth century and within ten years had captured all the Arab towns. These they held for a century, until the annexation of Portugal by Spain and the appearance in the Indian Ocean of other European commercial rivals weakened their hold on the coast. Little by little the Arabs thrust out the Portuguese and regained their influence. Portugal retained only the stretch of coastland between Cape Delgado and Delagoa Bay and this became the nucleus of the modern Mozambique. By the 1830s all coastal towns to the north, as well as the islands of Zanzibar and Pemba, were in the hands of the Sultan of Muscat, Seyyid Said. In 1840 Said moved his headquarters from Muscat to Zanzibar, the better to organize his East African trade in

24

ivory and slaves. During the first half of the nineteenth century the tribes of the East African interior organized their own long-distance caravans to the coast, and began to spread the coastal language, Swahili, inland as a *lingua franca*. By the 1840s and 1850s Arabs were building up-country settlements and endeavouring to secure control of the sources of ivory and slaves in Uganda, western Tanzania, and across Lake Tanganyika in what is now Zaïre. Meanwhile the importation of trade goods and particularly of firearms greatly enhanced the power of the rulers of the centralized lake kingdoms and afforded an opportunity in other areas for military leaders like Mirambo of Tanzania to carve out empires for themselves.

In the 1860s and 1870s the British, through their consul in Zanzibar, exerted pressure on Said's successor to restrict his slaving activities, while British philanthropy and patriotism prompted the exploration of the mainland. Livingstone, Burton, Speke, Grant, Baker, Stanley and Cameron were foremost in the enterprise. European traders and missionaries quickly followed the explorers and were caught up in a gathering, colonial vortex.[12] When Dr Karl Peters's new colony in Tanzania was ratified by Germany in 1885, Britain was aggrieved by this brutal incursion into an area in which she had been quietly pursuing commercial and humanitarian interests. The Imperial British East Africa Company was founded in 1887, and Uganda was annexed after a period of upheaval in which the Company's forces and rival Catholic and Protestant parties took part. During the unsettled period that preceded annexation more than thirty young Christian men died for their faith, and are now known as the Martyrs of Uganda.

At the turn of the century, therefore, East Africa consisted of three colonial territories: the Uganda Protectorate, British East Africa (later the Colony and Protectorate of Kenya) and German East Africa (now Tanzania, Rwanda and Burundi). Anxious to secure the headwaters of the Nile, the British pushed a railway from Mombasa through to Lake Victoria, while the Germans also constructed a railway from Dar-es-Salaam, their capital, to Ujiji on Lake Tanganyika. The British encountered considerable tribal opposition to the building of the railway, particularly from the Kalenjin, but the most serious threat to a colonial power was posed by the risings in German East Africa, first the rising of Abushiri in 1889, and then in the years after 1904 by the so-called Maji Maji rebellion, a politico-religious movement which affected large areas

25

in the east of the country. The Germans also encountered fierce opposition from the warlike Hehe tribe and their legendary leader Mkwawa, who even succeeded in annihilating a German invading force in 1891.

The First World War witnessed an East African campaign in which South African forces were brought up by sea and British and Belgian troops attacked German East Africa from three sides. The German colonial government capitulated in 1916, but the German commander von Lettow-Vorbeck succeeded in eluding the Allies right up until the time of the Armistice.[13]

After the war most of German East Africa (the modern Tanzania) was ceded to Great Britain under a mandate from the League of Nations and became known as Tanganyika Territory. In this way the whole of East Africa fell under one administering power, Britain. In Tanganyika and Uganda the British pursued a policy of so-called 'indirect rule', attempting to rationalize the traditional political systems and administer the country through native authorities. In Kenya, however, a policy of white settlement was followed. Even before the Second World War there were political associations and movements of protest in all three countries, influenced in a number of cases by the idealism and vocabulary of Christianity, if not actually articulated within African independent churches. The Second World War heightened African political consciousness to an unprecedented degree, and, in the case of Tanganyika, the new United Nations Organization demanded that there be clear progress towards self-rule. Soon after the war, Africans were introduced into the Legislative Councils of all three territories.[14]

In Tanganyika, Julius Nyerere founded the Tanganyika African National Union (TANU) in 1954, and in spite of the subsequent opposition of the United Tanganyika Party, started as a countermeasure by the government, won all the seats in the Legislative Council in the 1958 elections. In 1959, TANU ministers entered the government, and after the general elections of 1960, won again by TANU, Nyerere was asked to form a government. Under this government, internal self-rule was granted in 1961, and finally independence later in the same year. A year later the country was declared a sovereign republic, and in 1964 the United Republic of Tanganyika and Zanzibar came into existence under the new name of Tanzania. In 1967 the Arusha Declaration laid down a programme of African socialism, called in Swahili *ujamaa* or 'familyhood'. Under this programme *ujamaa* villages or collective farms have come into existence. Although TANU continues to be the sole, and ruling, party, broadly based elections are held regularly for seats in the National Assembly. An important recent project is the construction by the Chinese of a railway link from the central railway line to Zambia.

In Kenya, Jomo Kenyatta returned from Britain in 1946, after a fifteen-year stay, to take over the leadership of the Kenya African Union, an organization which had become the focus for Kikuyu nationalism. The KAU went from strength to strength, demanding an adequate representation for the African population in the government. This was opposed by the white settlers. Eventually in 1952, violence broke out, instigated by a politico-religious secret society known as Mau Mau, which had either the active or passive support of virtually all the Kikuyu. Few people, perhaps, sympathized with the depths of self-abasement to which some of the Mau Mau members descended, but the grievances—especially those concerning land—were felt by all. Atrocities were committed by both sides and the state of emergency did not finally end until 1960. During the emergency Kikuyu political activity was banned and Kenyatta and other leaders were imprisoned. In this situation, two political leaders emerged, Tom Mboya representing the Luo, and Ronald Ngala representing the Giryama and the peoples of the coast. After the Lancaster House Conference in 1960 which envisaged an African majority in the Legislative Council and the Government, two political parties came into being led by Mboya and Ngala. These were the Kenya African National Union (KANU) and the Kenya African Democratic Union (KADU). KANU united both the Luo and the Kikuyu, and James Gichuru accepted the presidency in the absence of Kenyatta. The 1961 elections gave the majority to KANU, which, however, refused to join the government until Kenyatta was released from prison. KADU entered the government and Kenyatta was released in the same year. In the following year Kenyatta and KANU won the general election and came to power when independence was granted to Kenya in December 1963. Tension between the Luo and Kikuyu grew within the KANU ranks until the Luo, Jaramogi Oginga Odinga led thirty members out of KANU to form the Kenya People's Party (KPU). The KPU lost the 1966 elections and was eventually proscribed after the riots which followed the assassination of Tom Mboya in 1969. The subsequent one-party elections were broadly based, but the advancing age of Kenyatta and the aftermath

27

of Mboya's death encouraged an abortive, Luo-inspired *coup* in 1971, and continue to give grounds for further anxiety.

In Uganda, the progressive strengthening and Africanization of the central Protectorate Government posed a serious threat to the special position of the Kingdom of Buganda. The Buganda parliament refused to nominate representatives to the Legislative Council and matters came to a head in 1952 when the Kabaka (King) of Buganda demanded separate independence for his kingdom. The exile of Kabaka Mutesa II enhanced his prestige and nullified the constitutional reforms which would have curbed his power. On his return the strained relations between Buganda and the central government virtually left the field open to two political parties. One was the Uganda People's Congress, led by Milton Obote, with support from outside Buganda. The other was the Democratic Party, led by Benedicto Kiwanuka, with support inside and outside Buganda, but with a mainly Catholic and anti-socialist appeal. The boycott by the Buganda nationalists gave the DP the majority in the elections of 1961 and Kiwanuka became Chief Minister. In order to defeat the DP, Obote allied with the Buganda nationalists and the UPC led Uganda to independence in October 1962, with Kabaka Mutesa as President and Obote as Prime Minister.

Then began the long struggle between Obote and Mutesa which ended in the constitutional crisis of 1966. After a bloody conflict Obote emerged supreme, in a new presidential-type of government. The Kabaka fled to Britain where he died in 1969, a state of emergency was declared in Buganda, five cabinet ministers were detained, and all the traditional kingdoms (including Buganda) were abolished. The assassination attempt against Obote in December 1969 afforded a pretext for the banning of the DP and the detention of Kiwanuka. However, Obote's new socialist policies began to alienate members of his own party and his detention of the Muslim leader Prince Kakungulu, brought about the opposition of the Muslim community. More important still was the alienation of the army by Obote's development of a para-military police and secret service. In January 1971, General Idi Amin Dada, a Muslim, took power in a military *coup d'état* and Obote went into exile in Tanzania. Amin declared the Second Republic of Uganda and became President of the military government. Kiwanuka was freed from detention and became Chief Justice.

Although the body of the Kabaka was brought back for burial in

Uganda, Amin showed no disposition to revive the traditional kingdoms. After an initial period of internal reconciliation and several armed conflicts within the army itself, Amin consolidated his position. This was further strengthened by two armed confrontations with Tanzania in 1971 and 1972 occasioned by the presence of Obote's supporters there, and by their return to Uganda as guerillas. The expulsion of non-citizen Asians in 1972 won Amin popularity within the country, but the move was widely condemned outside Uganda. The idea of placing the economy in the hands of 'Black Ugandans'—a process known in Uganda as the 'Economic War'—has also entailed the take-over of some British estates and businesses and the expulsion of some British residents. It has been generally a period of upheaval and tension, in which some cabinet ministers have defected, and prominent figures, such as Kiwanuka himself, have disappeared. The country is now returning to a greater measure of peace and stability.

4

Conservative pastoral societies

Few African tribes are so well known as the Masai of East Africa. With their striking physique and noble bearing, they are the obvious choice for the cover photo of a travel brochure or as a symbol of all that is romantic and singular about Africa. Pastoralism has a romantic appeal. The image of the warrior-herdsman—not unconnected with the Hamitic myth alluded to in the last chapter—evokes admiration. His independent spirit and apparent conservatism make him, in the eyes of the tourist, the survival of an Africa that is passing away, if it has not already disappeared. This popularity has given rise to a great many misconceptions about pastoralism in East Africa, which are partly due to the fact that the Masai themselves are not typical of East African pastoralists.

One of the misconceptions is that herdsmen are exclusively dependent on their stock—even on one single kind of stock, cattle.[1] In fact, most of the so-called pastoralist peoples of East Africa do a fair amount of cultivation as well as herding. Moreover, they are never dependent on a single kind of stock. They all possess a quantity of small stock, sheep or goats, and some even have other kinds of large stock, such as camels and donkeys. The Masai are untypical in that they do virtually no cultivation, but even they raise sheep as well as cattle.

Another popular misconception is that pastoralists are completely independent and self-sufficient. This is far from the case. In western Uganda and north-western Tanzania cattle-owning aristocracies exploit a class of conquered or client Bantu cultivators. Strictly speaking, these two-tiered societies are not usually classed as pastoral societies, but even in the societies which are more homogeneous, pastoralists are extremely dependent on neighbouring agricultural peoples and traders, both for food-stuffs and for necessities and valuables that are a part of their economy and culture. The Masai, themselves, although less obviously dependent on their neighbours, are served by their own class of serfs, the Ndorobo or Asi, who slaughter their animals for them, and by a clan of blacksmiths who forge their weapons and ornaments. The Masai have become increasingly dependent on traders who provide the iron and wire needed by the blacksmiths, and even certain skins, feathers and horns which are a part of Masai accoutrement.

Another misconception concerns the extent to which the physical environment determines a society in its choice of a pastoral economy. It has been said that pastoral societies deliberately limit their exploitation of the physical environment, and that they have rejected a number of choices open to them. It is true that, in the case of the Masai, the environment is equally suited to a hunting-gathering economy or an agricultural economy as to pastoralism. However, as we have already seen, such choices are not necessarily contradictory and many cattle-raising people are pastoral only in the sense that they give greater weight to stock-rearing than to agriculture. Even the Masai practise some hunting and gathering. They hunt animals to obtain skins for adornment and barter, and they are particularly fond of wild honey. Furthermore, although one would not wish to deny the weight of the accumulated choices which constitute a human social tradition, East African pastoralists live, for the most part, in 'marginal' areas in which obtaining a livelihood is difficult whatever economic choice is made. The environments vary a great deal, but it is clear that, if in some areas agriculture is precarious, pastoralism is also severely conditioned and limited. This applies especially to the movement of herds and settlements with which we must now deal.

One final misconception to be considered is the belief that pastoral societies are nomadic. In fact, although pastoralists are mobile to some extent, their movements are more limited than is popularly supposed. Many pastoralists never move their settlements at all. Their herds, on the other hand, may be constantly on the move from one grazing ground to another at a greater or lesser distance from the settlements. Sometimes rainfall and availability of grazing make a seasonal movement necessary, and cattle camps may have to be constructed at a considerable distance from the settlements. Even where the settlements are moved frequently, it is possible to plot a general pattern of movement, an ebb and flow that is more correctly described as 'transhumance' than as nomadism.

What is it, then, that characterizes the pastoral society in East Africa? Briefly, it is a type of society in which cattle are the central value in a whole culture-complex, and the basis of association in a complex of institutions, social, political and religious. Cattle are objects of interest in themselves, their hide markings and their horn shapes. They are the subject of praise poems and songs. They are the symbols employed in all public ritual. They are used to mark crises and transitions in people's lives and it is through cattle, and particularly the sacrifice of cattle, that they seek contact with the deity.[2] Cattle have an obvious economic value. They provide food in meat, milk and blood. Their fat is used as a cosmetic, their urine as a cleanser. Their hides are used for sleeping-skins, clothes and sandals, and their horns and hooves for containers. Where cultivation is practised, their droppings are used as manure. Cattle are used for the development of the family. Ties are established between family groups, and children are legitimated, through the exchange of cattle as bridewealth. Exchange of stock is the basis for a whole network of interpersonal relations outside the family, as well as being the normal expression of the relationship between kinsmen. As Michel Kayoya of Burundi has written: 'Man respects the cow. Like him, the cow is a relationship . . .'[3] This is true for groups, as it is for individuals. Cattle are objects of shared or divergent interest between groups, and this interest determines political relationships between them. Contiguous cattle-owning tribes become rivals, aspiring to a monopoly of the valued stock.

An important characteristic of East African pastoral societies is their high degree of social stratification. Social status is acquired in these societies, as in others, through age. But the acquisition of status is made explicit by communitarian rites of passage, and the societies are organized in terms of stratified age-sets, possessing public duties. Among the Jie and Karimojong of Uganda, for example, there are two generation-sets, a senior and a junior. Each generation-set is composed of five age-sets, having a depth of from five to six years, and composed, in turn, of a number of age-groups initiated annually. The responsibility of the senior set is mainly ritual, but the junior adults act as a disciplinary force within each descent group. Other peoples are more highly organized. The Nandi of Kenya, for example have a cyclical age-set system. There are seven recurring age-sets, each having a depth of fifteen years. The Masai of Kenya and Tanzania, however, have only three basic divisions of boy, warrior and elder. In common with the Nandi and Samburu of Kenya, the Masai warrior age-set has an important social and political function.[4] The status of warrior or *moran* (*murran*) was a means of prolonging adolescence in a polygamous society, where men delay marriage, and where there is necessarily some disparity in age between husbands and wives. It was also a means of canalizing adolescent rebelliousness for the good of society as a whole, and softening the chagrin the young men felt at losing their sweethearts who became the wives of older men. The young men acted as a military force and as a kind of police, living together and having a collective morality and allegiance. This kind of peer-group was autonomous, if conservative, and it fulfilled a recognized social role. Naturally, it is becoming more and more difficult to maintain such a warrior class in existence. Not only does the extension of school education threaten such a system, but close administration makes it virtually impossible for the warrior to fulfil his traditional role. It is doubtful if the *moran* can subsist forever on his earnings from tourist photographers, without eventually becoming affected by the behaviour and values of the tourists themselves.

The pastoralists of East Africa mostly inhabit the grassland corridor of eastern Uganda, western Kenya and north-central Tanzania; let us look at some examples. Much has already been said in this chapter about the Masai and little more need be added here. The basic social unit among the Masai is the household of an elderly father, his wives, his married sons and their families. In the compound each wife has her own, low hut, or *manyatta*. Cattle herding is carried out by the young men, under the direction of the married men, but the former (between the ages of sixteen and thirty) live apart, as we have seen, as warriors with their own kraal. The Ndorobo serfs provide the Masai with cereals and vegetables, and they also carry out the circumcision when young men are initiated into the warrior age-sets. A clan of priest-chiefs exists and these are consulted, particularly before war expeditions. The head of the clan is the paramount religious leader, who is highly respected for his powers of prophecy and intercession. With political and strategical ability, such a leader can give unity and direction to the action of the whole tribe through his prophecies.

Away to the west, in north-eastern Uganda are found the pastoral peoples of Karamoja District. Of these the Jie and Karimojong are well-known examples.[5] The Jie have a mixed economy of millet farming and animal husbandry and they have trade with foreign blacksmiths, pottery-makers and tobacco-growers. The country of the Jie is arid and wild, but there has been a growing stability of the population, leading to the foundation of more or less permanent settlements. These hamlets each represent a different clan, and a group of from one to eight such hamlets owns a grove in which they carry out ritual for rain-making. Settlements amalgamate into districts, also for rain-making and ceremonial functions, and it is the task of the senior elders to organize these ritual activities. The age-set system exists, therefore, mainly for ritual purposes.

In Jie the pastoral pattern is transhumant, and the movement is based on the fact that, after the rains, surface water and grass last longer in the west than in the east. When the rains are over, the herds move west. Only the young men, boys and a few women live in, and move with, the stock camps. The old men, women and children remain in the permanent settlements. The homestead consists of fenced yards for each wife in the compound, and the lowest social unit, which is represented by the homestead is the 'house', the association of independent full-brothers, sons of one woman. Although the women act as dairy-maids and are responsible for specially allocated milking stock, they cannot be the owners of cattle and they eventually come under the authority of their own sons. The women, however, have their own gardens, and decide what to grow there and how to dispose of the produce. The 'house-line' consists of a group of increasingly independent descendant houses, but the extended family has relatively little importance. What finally distinguishes one house from another is the fact of possessing a single residual herd. Bridewealth usually consists of fifty cattle and at least half of this number is found by the house. The remainder comes from kinsmen and stock-associates or the so-called bond-friends.

The Karimojong live to the south of the Jie and their pattern of settlement and movement is similar. Indeed the two peoples are closely related. Movement is extremely complex and only affects the camp herd, not the milking stock which remains at the settlement. All the herd-owners who share a single settlement may be said to form a single herding unit, loaning one another herd-boys and feed, and giving other kinds of mutual assistance. The camp-unit is made up of two or more herding units who combine to share a camp, and very often are bond-friends who have a stock-exchange contract. The camp group is the outcome of two or more camp-units combining for security against warfare and wild animals. Finally, we may speak of a camp-cluster in which a number of camps exploit a common grazing area or a common source of water. The age-sets and generation-sets have much the same functions as among the Jie.

The Turkana, across the Kenya border, are the eastern neighbours and traditional enemies of the Jie and Karimojong.[6] They have practically no agriculture and their nomadism is more thorough-going than that of the other groups we have considered. Not only do the herds move in search of grazing and water, but the very settlements themselves are moved. When the movement takes place, not all the neighbours move. Those that do, do not move in the same direction, nor do they reform again on their return. All that can be said is that individuals move within the limits of their geographical knowledge, and this results in some nineteen territorial sections, based on where people spend the wet seasons. The movement takes place between the plains and mountains. When the rains cease and the plains dry out, there is still a water-supply in the foothills of the mountains and a permanent supply of grass. The Turkana herd camels and donkeys as well as cattle and small stock.

The only distinct corporate group among such a mobile people is the nuclear family, consisting of a man, his wives and children and some other relatives who happen to be living with him. The wives have fenced yards like the Jie and Karimojong, but the married sons move away as soon as they can. The extended family, which is not residential, is responsible for mortuary ceremonies and other rituals. The individual is himself responsible for collecting bride-wealth from his kinsmen and stock-associates.

Between the pastoralists of the Karamoja area and the Masai of the Rift Valley lie a number of pastoralists who are more settled and more committed to agriculture, although their social organization possesses some of the features of the peoples already described. The Sebei of eastern Uganda, for example, grow sorghum and millet and are organized into age-sets, while the Nandi of Kenya's south-western highlands have also taken up agriculture, but continue their cyclical age-sets and their class of young warriors.[7]

The Masai extend into northern Tanzania, and the Arusha[8] who live to the west of them are known as the 'agricultural Masai'. In

35

spite of their Masai dialect and their dominant connection with the Masai, they have always been primarily sedentary cultivators, and were already cultivating before they moved to their present territory. They had little or no livestock from the beginning. The Gogo of central Tanzania, however, place a much greater emphasis on pastoralism and on the social and economic value of cattle.[9] For them, cultivation is decidedly secondary, and frequent droughts and famines cause considerable mobility of residence. The focal points of loyalty for the Gogo are the clan categories, linked, as they are, by joking partnerships and 'perpetual kinship'. All social ties are established through the exchange of cattle, and this is particularly true of marriage ties. The cattle-owning group, however, is not large enough to provide all the bridewealth and this necessitates wider co-operation. Bridewealth is high and is thus a function of large-scale social co-operation. The neighbourhood cluster of homesteads acts as a bridge between domestic kinship relations and the broader political and legal spheres, while the ritual area, with its officer, the *mutemi*, has a ritual and protective role.

As the title of this chapter implies, the pastoral societies of East Africa are frequently judged conservative and particularist. Although there is truth in this charge, it is very easy to overlook the special factors involved in modernizing these societies and integrating them into a modern, independent nation. Colonial governments tended to see the pastoral way of life as idle and an encouragement for mischief-making. Mobility rendered close administration difficult, if not impossible, and, in government opinion, there was a dangerous over-dependence on cattle. In some cases—Karamoja for example—military force was used to demarcate the pasture areas and stabilize the population. Apparently 'empty' lands were re-allocated to neighbouring tribes and a completely alien pattern of local administration was imposed which was the antithesis of the people's own system. Attempts were made to make the herds move westwards, rather than eastwards, for grazing, until an agronomist demonstrated that the western grasses lacked necessary chemicals and that the Karimojong were right to avoid them. Everywhere, fruitless attempts were made to interest pastoralists in agriculture and to detach them from their preoccupation with cattle. When independence came in the 1960s, the African administrators who replaced the British were even more embarrassed by the resistance and isolation of the pastoralists. Constant cattle-raiding from neighbouring tribes kept the rates of criminal homicide high. Moreover, many pastoralists looked upon clothing as a supplementary adornment of the human body, rather than as a covering demanded by rules of modesty. The nudity and cult of physique which made the pastoral peoples well-known throughout the world was acutely embarrassing for modern, independent governments attempting to project an image of modernity and civilization. Force was frequently used to police and clothe them, rendering them even more defensive and withdrawn.

Attempts to develop East Africa's pastoral resources came late. Bore-holes were dug, dams were erected, cattle were inoculated, stock was improved and cattle sales began. From an economic point of view everything was wrong with traditional methods of cattle raising.[10] Revenue was not the object. The growth of the herds was too slow and the herds contained an excess of males and over-age animals. The reproduction rate of the cows was mediocre, and meat and milk production were laughable when compared with results in European countries. Animals were poorly cared for, there were inadequate sanitary conditions, serious feed deficiencies, and an extremely high mortality rate among calves. Feed sources were seasonal or irregular and there was little or no idea of cultivating feed for cattle. If there was any interest in selective breeding it was not on the basis of meat and milk, but on the colour of the hide or the shape of the horns, factors of social or cultural importance.

When an entire culture or social system is based upon cattle as a symbol of social relationships and an object of sentiment, it is obviously extremely difficult to introduce a predominantly economic approach. The whole fabric of society is threatened, and this explains why the efforts to make an economic success of cattle-raising represent a more dangerous and a more subtle attack on the way of life of pastoral peoples, and demand a more sweeping revolution from them than is the case with other peoples. Moreover, with their overriding interest in 'sentimental' livestock raising, they are more highly specialized, and less prepared to adapt and diversify. Nevertheless, in spite of the slow rate of progress, there are clear signs that economics are prevailing over sentiment, and that cattle-sales are beginning to vie with cattle-exchanges. With this development it must also be admitted that the whole delicate balance of relationships between kinsmen and stock-associates is being upset and that

37

the social fabric of pastoral peoples in East Africa is being undermined. It remains to be seen whether the predominantly pastoral tribes can preserve something of their cultural tradition, as is the case with the Nandi and others who have a mixed economy.

5
Chieftain societies

If the man in the street knows nothing else about the traditional,
political institutions of Africa, he is nevertheless sure of one thing—
Africans are, or were, governed by chieftains or chiefs. The idea of
'chief' was strong in the minds of the British who colonized East
Africa, and the search for authentic chiefs was fundamental to the
British policy of indirect rule. 'Who is Chief?' was among the first
questions asked by the conquerors. That this question could have
had any one of a hundred meanings does not seem to have occurred
to the questioners. Equally, it could have had no meaning at all.
The English words 'chief' or 'chieftain' (and the Swahili word
sultani, with its Arab and Islamic overtones) suggest the political
rule of a single man, or the supreme command of a military leader.
We have already seen, in the last chapter, that such rulers or leaders
hardly existed in the pastoralist societies of East Africa. In many
other societies political and cultural identity was focused on an
individual who was, either wholly or mainly, a ritual officer, and even
where the political and military functions of the ruler were
more discernible, there were the problems of hierarchies of chiefs
and associations of chiefdoms. There were also striking differences
of degree among autonomous chiefs, as, for example between the
King of Buganda (Uganda) ruling nearly two million people, and
the Chief of Ubungu (Tanzania) ruling some 20,000. It is small
wonder, therefore, that many of those who put themselves forward
as 'chiefs' under British rule either did not meet the expectations of
the colonial government, or were regarded as imposters by those they
ruled.

That being so, it must be admitted that among many East African
peoples political organization takes on a symbolic form in the person

of a ritual leader or sacral ruler—varied examples of the so-called 'divine king', a concept first studied by Sir James Frazer.[1] That the institutions of divine kingship bear a remarkable similarity wherever they are found, is due more, perhaps, to sociological imperatives than to historical movements of diffusion, but the imagination of historians has been caught by divine kingship, and it has become the subject of grandiose theories. Professors Oliver and Fage have seen divine kingship as an outstanding feature of Negro or Sudanic kingship which spread southwards and westwards from the Upper Nile Valley—'. . . institutions', they say, 'were so similar that they must have derived from a common source.'[2] Earlier, Seligman had believed that Bantu divine kingship in East and Central Africa derived from the Pharaohs of Egypt, and, more recently, Mrs Meyerowicz has made a similar claim for the Ghanaian and Akan kingdoms of West Africa.[3]

Within East Africa such diffusionist theories have appeared more realistic, but even here the early claims have had to be modified in the light of recent research. From a discussion of the similarity of chiefly institutions in the Great Lakes region and western Tanzania, Oliver was led to consider the origin of this similarity in a movement of diffusion from the Lacustrine area.[4] He singled out four main institutions: the possession of special insignia, the use of royal fire, special rites connected with the death and burial of the chief, and the idea of divine kingship itself. As we shall see, the notion of divine kingship is a general one, and, as Frazer defined it, it always includes regicide or the fiction that the king descends living into the grave. An examination of royal insignia and of the use of royal fire reveals that there are various traditions which admittedly unite a number of ethnic groups, but which do not support the idea of a single movement of diffusion from the area of the Lakes. Rather, they suggest a number of influences, moving in different directions and converging in different places, resulting in different combinations. Such a picture is borne out by the analysis of chiefly traditions. Oral history shows us dynastic groups moving in many directions, leaving one area and settling in another, forming and re-forming alliances with other dynastic groups.

Furthermore, it has been suggested that the small-scale chiefdoms of western Tanzania, with their segmentation and their matrilineal institutions, represent an early phase in the development of the great kingdoms of the lake area, and that, although ultimately deriving from this area, conditions elsewhere did not favour their development into centralized states.[5] On the contrary, it is said, the chiefdoms simply proliferated as the population expanded. Although matrilineal institutions are an important structural feature of many of these chiefdoms, it is difficult to substantiate this hypothesis. Oral traditions, as we have seen, do not favour it, and in some instances it can be convincingly shown that the proliferation of chiefdoms accompanied a decline in the population. Indeed, the effective exploitation of a large area of bush, mainly through hunting and gathering, depended on the multiplication of centres, as did the holding of this area against the claims of rival, immigrant groups. The lake kingdoms are characteristic of the fertile regions where cattle or land comprise the royal patrimony. The multi-chiefdom societies characterize the less fertile regions where land is plentiful and populations sparse, and where the emphasis is less on the shifting cultivation that is carried out than on the forest pursuits of hunting and gathering. The more one studies the chieftain societies of eastern Africa, the less plausible appears the idea that there was a single phenomenon called 'chiefship' which was being passed from one ethnic group to another.

All kings are, by definition, sacral rulers. Their rule is supported by religious sanctions. Kings may also be priests or mediators in religious worship; but the divine king is something more. The divine king is somehow in himself divine—a living pledge of divine favour and success for his people. He reigns rather than rules, and he is the focus of innumerable rituals, rather than the repository of real power. Divine kingship is really a development of the function of the pastoralist 'priest-chief' who symbolizes in himself the will of a number of loosely organized political groups to co-operate at different moments. The office of the divine king has a wider relevance—to the whole ethnic group—and it is exercised more or less continually. Divine kingship emerges where the various political segments are loosely bound together by an organization devoid of any real political functions.[6] Political organization then takes on a symbolic form, but whether or not it develops into a centralized monarchy wielding real political power depends mainly on the availability of a royal patrimony.

One of the earliest analyses of African political systems, that made by Evans-Pritchard and Meyer Fortes, distinguished two main types: the kingdom with a centralized administrative organization

41

and the stateless society with no central government, a society in which the segmentary lineage system regulates political relations between the different social units.[7] In fact, this original division has proved too simple and a number of intermediate systems have since been discovered. One such system, that of the segmentary state, has been described by Southall for the Alur of north-western Uganda.[8] The Alur are a multi-chiefdom society, a power pyramid composed of many chiefdoms, culminating at the apex in a founder chiefdom. The proliferation of chiefdoms takes place as a result of the segmentation of the chiefly lineage. As the chiefdoms expand, their segments grow in number and chiefless peoples are assimilated peacefully at the periphery. Each chiefdom unit in the pyramid is a microcosm of the original founder chiefdom, and the latter exercises a decreasing control over them, the further away they are from the apex.

It must not be thought, however, that a state is segmentary only because it is composed of segmentary lineages. Segmentation is characteristic of all power competition, as M. G. Smith has pointed out, and a government takes on a segmentary form when segmentation pervades the whole administrative structure.[9] This segmentation may or may not coincide with lineage segmentation, which need not have any political significance. In western Tanzania there exist groups of peoples having a traditional political structure of chiefdom associations, and these associations are characterized by a segmentation which is only partially identifiable with lineage segmentation.[10] Such are the Nyamwezi, Sukuma, Kimbu, Konongo, and Galla (Tanzania), to mention but a few. Although the main impetus for the development of the associations has been the segmentation of an original chiefly lineage, a more important factor has been the challenge provided by invading alien groups. Sometimes an expanding chiefdom segmented through the peaceful or warlike assimilation of one of these groups. At other times segmentation was used by a sparsely populated chiefdom to counteract the threat of invasion, by multiplying the centres of operation in order to exploit the environment more effectively and so substantiate its claim to occupation.

In the segmentary state, typified by the Alur of Uganda, specialized political roles have developed between superordinate and subordinate segments, thus bringing a rudimentary administrative structure or pyramid into existence. At the apex, however, the roles are not so well developed, and there is nothing like a central government, or what may be strictly called a hierarchical structure. Among the multi-chiefdom societies of western Tanzania, such political roles are even less well developed and there is considerable competition between super-ordinate and subordinate segments. Among the Kimbu there is what may be called a 'cumulative opposition', based on priority of historical entry into the area, between the various associations of chiefdoms, but tension also exists among the component chiefdoms of the associations. The founder chiefdoms of the associations are, moreover, rivalled by their own offspring, which have become founders of chiefdoms in their turn, and there is scarcely a discernible apex to the pyramid. This tension weakens the pyramidal structure as a whole and renders the limited structural relations between adjacent segments more important than any more comprehensive control exercised at the apex. Relations between adjacent chiefdoms are limited to ritual duties, or to exceptional occasions provided by war or chiefly succession.

East Africa also provides us with examples of the single chiefdom society, or kingdom. Apart from the highly centralized kingdom which we describe below, there are two main kinds of single chiefdom society. One of these is the small, traditional chiefdom which has preserved its autonomy and which is virtually unattached to any association of chiefdoms or power pyramid. The other is the 'empire' created by military leaders or chiefs who deployed a patrimony, and were thus able to weld a number of smaller elements into some kind of political unity. The first type's survival is largely due to accidents of history and geography which have prevented it from being absorbed by more powerful neighbours and allies. In some cases the small, single chiefdom is the surviving core of an empire or hegemony which has since disintegrated. The small chiefdom of Ubungu in southern Tanzania has known a single ruler for most of its history. During the eighteenth century it was a prey to external influences and there was a lengthy period of usurpation of the chiefship by a foreigner. During the following century, the Bungu imitated the military techniques of the Ngoni, and allied themselves with the newly arrived Arabs who equipped them with firearms. Under Chief Kilanga I they raided far and wide, but met their match in the persons of the Sangu Chief Merere, and the Nyamwezi conqueror, Nyungu-ya-Mawe. Luckily for the Bungu, the empires of their powerful neighbours were ephemeral, and they managed to retain their own political identity up until modern times. The Sangu also survived as a single chiefdom after the collapse of their hege-mony.[11]

The Hehe of south-central Tanzania provide a good example of an empire that succeeded. In early times the country of the Hehe was the scene of numerous small migrations which resulted in a complex multi-chiefdom society. In the nineteenth century the political map of this area was completely changed by Munyigumba and Mkwawa, successive military leaders who welded these heterogeneous peoples into a warrior nation that subdued surrounding tribes and even defeated a German colonial army. These Hehe chiefs owed their success to a number of factors. Military victories gave them control over the sources of income, ivory, cattle and slaves, and the all-important trade goods, cloth and firearms which constituted their patrimony. Equally important was their ritual position and the possession of 'war medicine'—factors which assisted in the establish-ment of a Hehe war psychology.[12]

It was not until the nineteenth century, when people became aware of the commercial value of ivory, that chiefs in the woodland areas of East Africa were able to deploy a patrimony at all. The chief con-trolled the economy of his chiefdom, but he did not dispose of valued goods, and, although permission had to be sought from the chief before a piece of bush could be cleared, land was too cheap a commodity in those infertile and sparsely inhabited areas to consti-tute a patrimony. Land was virtually unlimited and the amount of land a man could farm depended on the amount of land he could clear. Cattle, as a patrimony, were also ruled out by the presence of the tsetse fly. Ivory had no traditional value, but it became, in the nineteenth century, a bargaining counter for the new valuables which were the fruit of long-distance trade. Chiefs and their families were foremost in the organization of this trade and they had a virtual monopoly of its profits, thus enabling them to extend their influence. Among the trade goods, guns and gunpowder played an important part. They not only made the hunting of elephants more efficient, but they also allowed chiefs to set up a well-armed force, with the help of which they could extend their monopoly and enlarge the scale of their operations.

Nyungu-ya-Mawe, the Nyamwezi adventurer-chief who built up an empire in west-central and southern Tanzania, affords a good example of this.[13] His conquests were motivated mainly by the desire to control the collection and disposal of ivory and the chiefs he subjugated by force were deprived of this right. By depriving them of the ability to deploy a patrimony, Nyungu was robbing the subject chiefs of all effective political power, and ultimately of their role as ritual leaders. Unlike the more famous Mirambo, who relied on military action almost exclusively to control his subject chiefs and whose empire began to disintegrate within a few days of his death, Nyungu set up a political structure of his own. This consisted of officials directly responsible to himself alone who policed the conquered chiefdoms and were the receivers of all ivory. These officials received their share of the booty and profits, and any insubordination on their part, especially pretence to chiefship, was ruthlessly punished. Nyungu thus rationalized a large section of the economic and political map of western Tanzania, turning it into a vast and efficient machine for the collection and disposal of ivory. It is not surprising that his empire survived his death by more than a decade and was only dismantled by the German colonial administration.

In the fertile and densely populated regions to the north, west and north-west of Lake Victoria a patrimony was readily available from earliest times in the shape of land and cattle. In the Kingdoms of Buganda and Bunyoro (Uganda) for example, local administration was strictly tied to a land benefice.[14] A subordinate chief received office through the grant of an area of populated land, and it was understood that he was responsible for its inhabitants and would support himself from their tribute. He, in his turn, would give tribute to the king by whose favours he held office. In this way the kingdom was governed through the granting of estates to appointed officials. In other kingdoms cattle were an additional benefice. In both Bunyoro and Ankole the king was held to be the ultimate owner of all cattle. He could take or grant cattle at any time, and he could tax all herds. In Ankole (Uganda) and the so-called Hinda states of north-western Tanzania there was even a caste system by which the cattle-owning Hima caste ruled the agricultural Iru caste who were bound to them in various ways. Chiefship, or indeed—as it may be more properly called in this case—kingship, was exercised in these areas on a far larger scale than elsewhere in East Africa. Moreover, it developed in varying degrees a far more centralized structure, leaving a difficult legacy for the modern nation-states which have succeeded the kingdoms.

While on this topic of the lake kingdoms, one important cultural fact must be mentioned, namely the Chwezi-Swezi traditions.[15] The

Chwezi are held to have been the rulers of ancient Kitara, the kingdom which was later replaced by the modern lake kingdoms, and the founders of the Hinda states. The historical content of these traditions is a matter for debate, but Chwezi traditions have had a profound influence on the cultures of western Uganda and western Tanzania, and they constitute one of the best attested examples of cultural diffusion from the lake region. These traditions characterize a complex of ancestral and spirit possession cults in the lake kingdoms, the Hinda states, and in Uha, Usumbwa, Usukuma and Unyamwezi. The legends and songs of the Swezi spirit possession cult in Usukuma and Unyamwezi have clearly been influenced by the Chwezi traditions of the lake kingdoms, although it has adopted medical techniques from Islamic spirit possession cults coming from the coast. In southern Unyamwezi and in Ukimbu the Swezi cult yields to the Migawo spirit possession guild, which, although it centres on beliefs of south-western origin and employs the coastal techniques already mentioned, continues nevertheless to sing the Swezi songs while their meaning goes unremembered. This is probably the most southerly limit of the Chwezi-Swezi influence.

Mention has been made of insignia and in this connection one can note several items which unite a number of societies with chiefly traditions. The royal symbolism of the lion is widespread, and so is the use of the drum as a royal emblem. However, towards the south the horn is of equal or greater importance. Also spreading from the south, is the tradition of the white conus-shell disc-emblem worn by chiefs on their foreheads, and sometimes on their wrists and ankles. These shells emanate from the east African coast and their use seems to have been pioneered mainly by the Kimbu and Sumbwa in the early nineteenth century. They have a solar or astral significance.

Chiefship, in its various forms and with its various traditions and institutions, characterizes mainly the western regions of East Africa. Elsewhere, political structures appear to be looser and more complex, varying from councils of elders, in societies that are more or less stratified, to highly fragmented situations with a multiplicity of dynastic groups and ritual officers. British administrators attempted, in their own way, to rationalize the multi-chiefdom societies and to develop a recognizable chiefship among peoples without chiefs. The concept of the 'paramount chief' ruling over a federation was a favourite one. In Tanzania, paramounts were created for the Chagga and for federations in Unyamwezi, Usukuma and Ukimbu. In other places, councils of chiefs were established. In general, the character of the chief was radically altered under colonial rule. He became a tool of the central administration, absorbed in tax matters, in court work, and in correspondence. He no longer fulfilled the social or economic expectations of his people. Rather, he taxed them without being the obvious channel of economic and social benefits.

In the lake kingdoms of Uganda, the British found a well developed native administration, but even here the same problems were present: the transformation of the county and parish chiefs into tax-collectors and court-holders, and the reconciliation of a handful of absolute monarchs, erstwhile rivals and enemies, to each other and to a central, federal-type administration. The Kingdom of Buganda was especially favoured, since the British extended their rule with its help, subjugating other parts of the country with the help of the Ganda and imposing an administrative structure on them which was based on that of Buganda. It was natural that such a proceeding should bring about considerable resentment, and that an independent government should decide to abolish the kingdoms. In the event, it was easy enough to depose the kings and to create a superficial political unity, but it was harder to bridge the underlying divisions between the groups formerly ruled by them. The lower levels of chief were retained and integrated into the district structure which re-placed the kingdoms. This was easy enough to do in an area where such officials had been appointed and had not ruled by hereditary right. Moreover, the grant of freehold land to particular individuals by the colonial government helped to detach the office of chief from the granting of an estate.

In Tanzania a more radical policy was both possible and desirable. The paramounts quickly faded into oblivion before all chiefs were deposed as government executives in 1963 and an entirely new admin-istrative structure introduced, comprising executives at district, divisional and village levels. Chiefs, however, continue to exercise some moral authority, and in multi-chiefdom areas, where adminis-trative 'villages' are extensive, chiefs are still in demand as unofficial village headmen.

In Kenya alone there has been virtually no change in the status of the chief, probably because the chief in Kenya was largely an arti-ficial creation by the British and was introduced with fewer conflicts and misunderstandings. Local chiefs were a new administrative concept and owed little to traditional political structures.

47

6

Urbanization

Towns are a relatively recent phenomenon in East Africa. Unlike many parts of West Africa with the possible exception of Mengo (Kampala), the region possessed no ancient metropolitan cultures, with temple or palace complexes and traditions of market trading. Only in the Islamic culture of the coast was there any early experience of town life. The Arab city-ports of Lamu, Malindi, Mombasa and Kilwa, and the island emporium of Zanzibar possessed a highly developed urban culture in the middle ages, but, although they conducted trade with the peoples of the hinterland, they had virtually no influence on the interior of East Africa, their position became more and more precarious, attacked both by land and sea. The long-drawn-out struggle with the Portuguese seafarers, and the depredations of warlike tribes such as the Zimba and Galla (Kenya) were inhibiting factors. The ruins of Gedi, near Malindi in Kenya, give the visitor some idea of the achievements of this urban civilization, but they are also a commentary on its vulnerability—in this case, to attack by the Galla. The spread of towns only became possible in the nineteenth century with the opening up of the interior by Arabs from Zanzibar, and one of the first towns to be founded by them in the interior was Tabora in 1852.

Towns first began to spring up along the lines of communication and their first reason for existing was the long-distance trade operated by the Arabs. The Sultan of Zanzibar had a tenuous hold over these centres, but they did not become centres of administration in any real sense until colonial power was established. Thereafter, the urban centres multiplied, primarily as headquarters of local administration, with the majority of town dwellers engaged in administrative and agricultural services to the surrounding countryside. East

African towns are non-industrial. There are no great mining towns comparable to those of South Africa or the Copperbelt, and the economically precarious character of mining in East Africa has produced little more than settlements or camps. Equally, there are no manufacturing towns and, although factories are everywhere being developed, it is only a small percentage of the urban population that is employed in them. The major cities and towns contain about a quarter of the national total of wage-earners, and of these, nearly half are employed in the public services, the remainder being divided between industry and commerce.

The fact that towns in East Africa are administrative and non-industrial explains both the rate and the pattern of urban growth in recent years. Growth is uneven and, while some towns are increasing rapidly, others are hardly increasing at all, or are even in decline. The most obvious examples of rapid urban growth are the 'super-cities', Nairobi (Kenya), Dar-es-Salaam (Tanzania) and Kampala (Uganda). Nairobi has a population of about half a million, while Kampala has something like a quarter of a million inhabitants. The population of Dar-es-Salaam is now well over a quarter of a million. Other towns, though considerably smaller, still retain considerable administrative and organizational importance. The ports of Mombasa (Kenya) and Tanga (Tanzania), both at railheads, are obvious examples; on the other hand, other old coastal towns, such as Malindi (Kenya) and Bagamoyo (Tanzania), while retaining some touristic significance, are of much less importance. Up-country towns such as Nakuru in Kenya, Dodoma and the lakeside town of Mwanza in Tanzania, and Jinja and Mbale in Uganda, are important both as administrative centres and because they are situated on important lines of communication. In the case of Jinja and Mwanza fairly important manufacturing centres have also grown up in the township.

However, there is nothing comparable to the extraordinary growth of the super-cities, Nairobi, Dar-es-Salaam and Kampala.[1] Nairobi City is increasing at twice the rate of growth of the total national population; Dar-es-Salaam at three times the rate; while Kampala's growth rate must be placed somewhere between the two. Growth in these cities reached its peak in the ten years following political independence, the decade of the 1960s, and there are indications that it is already tapering off. What provided the impetus for this rapid growth? As we have seen, we are dealing with non-industrial, administrative centres, and it seems that the growth must be attributed to the enormous expansion of government and public services, consequent upon independence. The super-cities are essentially a power phenomenon, centres from which a relatively small national population is tightly controlled. Culturally, the urban mentality may not reach very far outside these East African cities, but in terms of political control they are crucial for the entire country. The organs of mass media emanate from the super-city, and, while the impact of the radio on local cultures is a matter for discussion, its political impact is highly significant. The events of 25 January 1971 in Uganda showed conclusively how control of the super-city and its national amenities was the key to control of the whole country. It was sufficient to secure the capital and to make this fact known by means of the radio for a change of government to take place almost without a blow.

In spite of this, the growth of the super-city is not necessarily economic and it is also, in large part, the consequence of increasing unemployment and underemployment. It has not been unknown for a city's population to increase when at the same time its labour force was actually declining. This happened in Kampala between 1958 and 1961. The cities are swollen with refugees from rural distress who earn and learn little in town, and whose presence there reduces the manpower available for agricultural development. Governments are certainly becoming more and more aware of this over-urbanization problem and are trying to counteract it, both by laws that curb city growth and by plans to site industrial projects more evenly in the country. Squatters are being evicted, vagrants rounded up, stringent planning rules enforced. In parts of Nairobi the battle between police and squatters is seemingly interminable. In the notorious Mathare Valley, for example, squatters are so well organized that they can dismantle their shanties at daybreak and re-erect them at nightfall!

The geography of the city reflects its character of power phenomenon. The centres of power, the desirable, residential areas and the shopping centres are situated on the high ground, while the low-income areas lie on the city outskirts and in the swampy, lower ground.[2] It is here, in the valleys, that the greater part of the urban population lives, carrying out allotment farming, indulging in market trading, and living generally in quasi-rural fashion. Unlike cities in the western world where the slums are located in the longer established centres, with their outmoded housing and sanitary facilities, in the newer, East African cities the slums are more likely to be located outside the city. Although the number of committed towns-men is steadily growing, bad conditions allied with unemployment are a factor contributing to the transience of the population.

Transience is certainly a major characteristic of East African urban populations. Swantz has even suggested that 20 per cent of Dar-es-Salaam's population changes every year, but even if the change is not as great as this elsewhere, it is certainly significant.[3] Transience is a major factor of difference between East African towns and towns in the western world. Besides bad urban conditions, there are other reasons which draw urban dwellers back to the countryside, or which encourage them to commute between town and country. Unlike the western countryman who comes to town, the African countryman comes not as a wage-earning agricultural labourer, but as the farmer of his own land, land which he cannot alienate, and which is the main source of income for the family community to which he belongs. This income is to be supplemented by the wage he earns in town. Again, he may come to town specifically as a 'target worker', working to achieve a particular target in earnings, in order to spend it on a project at home, the development of his farm, bridewealth, etc.

Parkin's distinction between 'host' and 'migrant' is a useful one.[4] Each of the East African cities is situated within a well defined tribal area, the people of which are the hosts. In Nairobi the hosts are the Kikuyu; in Dar-es-Salaam, the Zaramo; in Kampala, the Ganda. The hosts represent a more stable element in town. Their proximity to their tribal homeland allows them a foot in both camps, as it were. Although they may have farms outside the city and may have fairly frequent contact with their family and with their rural com-munity of origin, they are in many ways more exposed to urban in-fluences and may more easily subscribe to new ideals and values. Casual unions tend, for example, to be more frequent among them.

The migrant, on the other hand, has his homeland further away. For him, the link with his tribal area and with his community of origin cannot be taken for granted. Family ties are important for him and he is more attached to traditional institutions and values. He may form a temporary liaison with a host girl, but by preference the partner he takes belongs to his own ethnic group and she will eventually become his wife. In East African cities the sex-ratio is generally far from equal, the men outnumbering the women by a very wide margin. Town girls have a bad reputation and men, whether host or migrant, usually hope to form a stable union with a country, rather than a town, girl. Men in towns marry late, not much before the age of twenty-five, and by middle age they have had four or five living partners. Most town dwellers are under the age of thirty and about a third are between the ages of fifteen and twenty. Small children however, tend to be relatively few, and parents often send growing children to the tribal homeland to be brought up by relatives there.

As we noted in the first chapter, the transformation of the tribe is a continuous process in which urbanization plays its part. The African townsman, with his own cultural background, has to meet new urban needs and fabricate new relationships in town. In East Africa, it must be confessed, the city offers a favourable milieu for tribal cleavages. Newcomers to town gravitate towards the 'tribal village' in the first stage of their urban initiation. Such villages are found in the low-income areas where there is a large number of unemployed. Later on, if the new townsman succeeds in obtaining a stable job, particularly if he is employed in one of the public services, he is able to move to a housing estate provided by the department that employs him, or to one of the higher income locations. These are essentially multi-tribal. Moreover, the wage-earner begins to mix with members of other ethnic groups at work and on the way to work. In his leisure moments at his location, he still manages to find, and mix with, members of his own tribe, as a matter of choice. Tribal influences remain strong with him in every choice he makes, and a great many unions and associations, set up on a tribal basis, exist to help him in moments of crisis or urgent need.

In many ways traditional culture co-exists with urban culture, or finds new scope within the latter. In many ways, too, it must be modified to suit the new conditions of life in town. At the domestic level and at the level of basic values, the African townsman remains under the influence of his own tradition. Human traditions and symbols of ethnic loyalty can be very strong indeed. An example is provided by the city-dwelling Gisu, who are some 150 miles from their homeland but who regularly perform the circumcision cere-monies in urban and peri-urban Kampala. Swantz found in Dar-es-Salaam that the host tribe, the Zaramo, had many cultural links with the surrounding countryside.[5] Besides the periods of harvesting and planting, when Zaramo women were absent from town for long periods, there were absences for puberty rituals and circumcision, and a large percentage of Zaramo women returned to their home villages to give birth to children. The majority of Zaramo are still buried in the rural areas to which the corpses of those who die in town are transported. Inevitably the communitarian rituals of the past suffer as a result of urbanization. They are curtailed and celebrated by a very much reduced community, often the family alone. The more individualistic rituals of power, however, seem to flourish in the urban situation and to arouse an immense amount of interest.

Witchcraft studies have shown that the pattern of witchcraft accusation in society follows the patterns of conflict and potential enmity that exist between people in the same social stratum. Town life is certainly not without conflict. People find themselves living next door to strangers, even persons of other ethnic groups. They also find themselves in fierce competition with others for jobs, for promotion, for housing. Such conflicts are frequently worked out in terms of witchcraft accusation. Then there are the many problems of a new and complex urban life, the need to be successful in business, the need to pass examinations and interviews, the need to escape the legal consequences of malpractice and so on. On top of all these comes the need for security in traditional terms and the need for a sense of continuity with traditional life. Whole areas of experience exist, certain diseases for example, which, according to most people's opinion, escape the control of European science and technology.[6] In Dar-es-Salaam Swantz estimated that there were 700 diviners operating, sharing 10,000 consultations between them daily, 56 per cent of which involved witchcraft accusation.[7] In Kampala, Rigby and Lule found highly organized and successful diviners who had adapted their beliefs and apparatus to suit the stresses and conditions of modern life.[8] New spirits had been discovered to deal with modern situations and procedures were carried out quickly and smoothly to cater for the very large number of clients produced by the urban situation. Many of these clients were wealthy businessmen and government officials. The urban population in general remains interested and impressed by such rituals of power. I well remember a dramatic instance of this which took place in Kampala in December 1970. For several hours the main street of Kampala City was blocked by a crowd of close on 5,000 people, defying all attempts of police and military to disperse them. They had gathered to verify a witchcraft case in which, it was alleged, an adulterer had been bewitched, in the very act of copulation, by his lover's irate husband. It was said that the guilty pair were unable to separate!

Obviously, with only a selection of its members residing in town, the African family community has to improvise and adapt. In spite of this, it proves quite resilient. Although it is subject to strong pressures, it manages, in many cases, to function as an economic unit with a system of mutual expectations and trust as the basis for credit. Leslie found a 'web of kinship ties criss-crossing the town' in Dar-es-Salaam, and the basic unit consisted of fairly close relatives—cousins, uncles, nephews.[9] The newcomer, arriving in town, was heavily dependent on such relatives until he could fend for himself and become, in his turn, a benefactor for his kinsmen. Kinship and ethnicity count for a very great deal in the East African city. People look for job opportunities for their relatives and fellow tribesmen. They lodge them and feed them and help them in moments of crisis, when they are sick or in trouble. A great deal of their earnings is paid out in the form of school fees for their young brothers and sisters and even more distant relatives. Probably, most successful townsmen are building a house in their home village, or in the peri-urban areas. This house, which often boasts a great deal of exterior ornamentation, is the symbol of their achievement. It is also the family home and is generally sited on land farmed by the family.

Although the small circle of fairly close relatives offers security in the urban situation, where structures are broad and alien, tribe is probably more important ultimately than family. In a multi-tribal situation, tribal allegiance obviously comes to mean more. The tribal association exists to cope with the larger social scale of urban living. Foreign nationalities can even function like tribes, and one finds the 'Kenyans' or the 'Rwandese' in Kampala interacting on the same basis with the Uganda tribes. Members of the host tribe, on the other hand, have less need for tribal associations, since their own tribal structures are available and sufficiently elaborate to meet the occasion. In the rural areas the ethnic groups had their own experience of personal networks based on cattle exchanges or on other forms of mutual assistance. In the town such networks are mainly informal, focused very often on the bars, beer-halls and night-clubs. Such places are very numerous, and their names, as well as the songs and dances performed there, reflect a new culture that owes much both to African tradition and to the ideals served by the mass-produced leisure products coming from the western world.

Although town-dwelling African women have a bad reputation, this is not entirely justified.[10] The loss of the roles they played in rural society may mean a corresponding loss of status; however, new, urban roles can bring new status. In town there is a growing opportunity for the businesswoman and the woman who is a property owner. Probably economic emancipation counts for more than educational emancipation. The educated woman is still rare, and she belongs to the small élite of the higher classes and professions. The woman who is successful in town is the ordinary practical woman, transplanted from the rural to the urban context. It is commonly said in East Africa that prostitution and loose living are evils that have been brought from Europe. In fact, they are endemic to the demography and conditions of the African town. The fact that there are relatively few women in the towns, and that it is men who form the vast majority of wage-earners, encourages women to seek material rewards and higher standards of life by entering into successive unions with men. Seemingly also, towns attract barren women. Fertility is low in East African towns, and while barrenness is often an unbearable reproach in the rural areas, in towns it can be a distinct advantage. A pregnancy might embarrass the male partner and cause him to terminate the relationship. Another factor is the unequal distribution of women among the tribes represented in town. Host women are more numerous than women of migrant groups, yet migrant men are unwilling to marry them. Temporary liaisons, therefore, are the only way of satisfying their sexual needs.

In East African towns, as has been noted, there is a high proportion of teenagers. These are chiefly boys. Many of them are students attending government and private secondary schools. In Nairobi and Kampala, in particular, private schools abound and students lodge in poor conditions, often taking part-time jobs to help make ends meet. Probably, however, the majority of these youths are seeking employment and are in and out of temporary jobs. The more enterprising and educated among them may attend evening classes to try and acquire some qualifications, but a large number remain frustrated and a prey to delinquency. The youth is probably the main consumer of mass-produced leisure and is strongly influenced by western cinema, 'pop' songs and fashions. The leisure culture of East African cities is mainly—as elsewhere in the world—a youth culture. However, although western influences have come in for strong criticism and even censure from the ruling powers, urban youth in East Africa has in fact made its own selections and adaptations and created its own distinctive symbols.

The short-term desire to participate in the pleasures offered by town-life has a great deal to do with the increase of violent crime in East Africa's large cities. Violent robbery is becoming increasingly well organized and the violent robber or *kondo* (as he is called in Kampala) is typically a well dressed, suave young man, who carries a revolver. Cars and large sums of cash are the most frequent objectives. The violent robber is not a poverty-stricken desperado, so much as a young man who has tasted the pleasures which the town has to offer and who has discovered that crime is a short-cut to obtaining and maintaining the style of life he enjoys. The law-abiding public has reacted in panic to the increase in crime. The anonymous criminals of the city represent a much more sinister threat than the occasional violence that takes place in the rural areas, and it is a threat posed to the whole edifice of urban culture with its system of incentives and rewards. In all three countries, Uganda, Tanzania and Kenya, draconian legislation has been passed with little or no effect. This has been realized in Tanzania, where the laws sentencing certain categories of thieves to corporal punishment have recently been repealed. As long as detection remains inefficient, deterrent sentences are completely unrealistic, and even if detection were improved, the result of such sentences would probably be merely that criminals would descend to even more violent extremes.

The town still remains something of a paradox in contemporary East Africa. It is at once an economic asset and an economic parasite. It possesses enormous political importance, yet it mirrors, rather than resolves, the cultural and structural heterogeneity of the nation it serves. However, in spite of these contradictions, an East African urban culture is beginning to make its appearance, and traditional society is slowly coming to terms with urbanization.

7

The rural revolution

Spectacular though the fact of urbanization is in Africa, it is now being realized that a far more important revolution is sweeping through the rural areas.[1] As was noticed in the last chapter, East African towns exist very largely to provide services to a countryside engaged almost wholly in agriculture. In a country like Tanzania, for example, 96 per cent of the population is engaged in agriculture. The realization has come that the economic development of East African countries means, in fact, rural development, and there has accordingly been a marked shift in emphasis towards this in the various development plans adopted during the past decade. The social changes wrought in the countryside affect a larger number of people in the long run, and, as has been seen, many even among the urban population are migrants from rural areas, still very much attached to their homeland, to which many ultimately return.

Some people have stressed urban influence as the major factor in the changes taking place in rural East Africa, and the towns are certainly important centres of planning and dominance. Yet one cannot attribute all that is taking place in the countryside to the spread of an urban mentality. That is altogether too naïve an explanation. The rural revolution is creating a modern rural mentality. It is directed towards the creation of new, but typically rural, structures, and to the betterment of social life in rural areas. Rural development is no longer defined merely in monetary terms, or terms of material output; it is now socially defined as aiming at an improvement in the quality of life, in health, nutrition, social services, education, and the involvement of the family and the community. Many bold experiments are taking place and there has been an impressive increase in research.

East Africa has shared to some extent in the so-called 'Green Revolution', the critical, and sometimes dramatic, increase in productivity which has affected so many areas of the non-western world. Unfortunately, this rise in productivity has been offset by other economic factors. In the ten years following the granting of political independence to East African countries, 1960-70, the exports of developing countries increased by 7·5 per cent, but their share in world trade fell from 21 per cent to 17 per cent. In agricultural trade the drop was, surprisingly enough, even greater—from 40 per cent to 33 per cent, a fall of 7 per cent.[2] East Africa has had her share in the disappointment. The output of major crops such as coffee, sisal and tobacco has risen dramatically but it is not East Africa that decides the world's need for these commodities or dictates their price. Fluctuations in the world market and the diminishing need of western countries for raw materials have given the promises of government planners to raise incomes and standards of living a hollow ring. After a dangerous fall in the balance of payments, East African governments have acted to curb imports, especially in what are deemed luxury goods. The result has been that the East African peasant has sometimes ceased to hope for the higher incomes promised if he produces for the export market, and has even begun to lose incentive to produce for the local cash market where his choice of trade goods is severely limited. Corruption and inefficiency have also sometimes added to a lack of credibility in the structures set up for agricultural development and marketing.

Fortunately, East Africa is reasonably fertile and can satisfy her own food requirements fairly easily. Today the sights have been set consciously lower. Particularly in Kenya and in Tanzania the emphasis has been on self-help development projects. Self-reliance is as important as raising incomes or increasing employment and training opportunities. While contributing to a national economy, peasants are being encouraged to pursue local community objectives, to build for a better social life in their own communities. The growing importance of a money economy and the decision to take local objectives into account in rural development have had profound and positive consequences for social life which justify use of the term 'revolution'. New forms of competition and co-operation have come into existence, new roles and statuses, a greater social mobility, a larger measure of individual responsibility and the demand for a more personal approach.

In the past there has not only been the problem of the migrant worker denuding the countryside of manpower and going to urban areas in search of salaried employment, there has also been the problem of 'élitist' education. Schools have not been confined to urban areas. As a result, in the first place, of missionary endeavour and, in the second place, of vigorous government programmes, schools have sprung up everywhere. Every village or large settlement has its own primary school today and there is an increasing number of secondary schools, both government and private. Probably more than half of the child population gets some schooling, even if a relatively small number go from primary to secondary school. In the eyes of most rural-dwelling parents the school is the gateway to a new world, a world of salaries and higher standards of living, a world of real power and influence in society. The greatest prestige attaches to the white collar worker.

Such an attitude has led to widespread disillusion and unrest. To begin with, the education system has had too many casualties. A system geared to produce an élite has to be highly selective, and many are those who fall by the wayside, their education incomplete. Employment simply does not exist for all school leavers, and one may even find university graduates, Higher Certificate and School Certificate school leavers all competing for the same job. At the lower levels the disappointed school leaver finds that his education is a handicap, rather than an advantage, when he realizes that there is no alternative to becoming a peasant farmer. His schooling has created needs and awakened desires that cannot be fulfilled. In the villages one may meet young farmers who are even losing the skills they acquired at school, such as literacy skills.

The problem of 'élitist' education is being met in a number of ways. To some extent efforts are being made to make education, particularly at the lower school levels, more realistic and orientated to a rural society. Not only is a respect for agriculture instilled into the children, but a spirit of self-giving and service is inculcated through school self-help projects. Tanzania has, perhaps, gone further than the other East African countries along this road of re-orientating the education system to fit in with rural development plans, and we shall have more to say about this subject of education in general in a later chapter. Another contribution to the solution is to make the local school multi-functional and to give it a place in the whole scheme of local community development. The school is an obvious organ of influence for government. Finally, the gradual build-up of social services in the countryside, the creation of structures for the training and supervision of people engaged in every aspect of development, demands educated personnel. Although urban areas remain powerful centres of attraction, education no longer leads exclusively to the town or city. Opportunities are increasing for educated people to play their part in the countryside where leadership is at a premium in this moment of structural and organizational change.

The estate or plantation still occupies an important place in the economies of East African countries. In the past, estates, particularly those which produced sugar, sisal, or cloves, employed seasonal or short-term migrant labour. This practice has had consequences comparable to those of urbanization: transience, bad conditions, ethnic rivalry, decline of the family, and so forth. On the whole, although people travelled vast distances to become short-term wage-earners on such estates, they had little ultimate interest in a job which took them away from their own homeland. In the first quarter of the twentieth century when migrants streamed down to the sisal plantations in eastern Tanzania, they returned with songs, ritual techniques (particularly in the area of spirit possession) and comic Swahili names which reflected a new, coastal world of money and trade goods. Structurally however, the rural societies of their respective homelands in the interior were untouched. As the years went by, the system of short-term contract labour gave way to the use of more permanent workers and the setting up of compounds or villages where workers could live with their families. Such a system resembles the rural re-settlement scheme, except in so far as the inhabitants are specialized labourers working for a company or state corporation, rather than settlers working and speculating on their own behalf.

Rural re-settlement schemes, sometimes known as 'villagization' were the first alternative to the estate or plantation. These schemes attempted to concentrate farmers and producers, so as to allow for greater supervision and training, as well as to make for closer government administration and easier and more effective organization of the social services. Although most African peasants probably value their independence and prefer to live and work in their own home areas, some have seen an advantage in moving to one of these settlements. Usually it was the prospect of assistance in getting started, the attraction of high incomes or the promise of facilities such as piped water or even electricity which lured them to the settlement. Where a settlement simply involves the re-grouping of farmers within their own homeland, it is obvious that there are fewer social problems. When, however, it involves the migration of settlers over long distances to make up a community of varied ethnic backgrounds one is up against all the problems of the host-migrant opposition once more. In many cases, the idea of re-settlement corresponds to a plan for developing a backward, or hitherto unexploited, area and this, inevitably, means bringing in large numbers of migrant settlers.

Perhaps it is still too early to speak of the success or failure, in social terms, of villagization experiments. However, it is apparent that for the migrant the settlement is an altogether artificial creation. It is his place of work, his source of income, but it hardly caters for his social needs. There is little or no social life in the settlement itself and there is not the compulsion that exists between neighbours of a single ethnic group to celebrate each other's family events—births, deaths, marriages, and so on. Marriages are almost exclusively between people of the same ethnic group, but these are either secondary marriages or marriages of younger family members who are not householders. It is a common entry qualification to the settlement that the prospective settler be married already, and, understandably enough, polygamy offers distinct advantages to a settler who needs as many pairs of hands as he can get to help in the development of the land entrusted to him. A settlement scheme has its own structures of authority and its own peculiar politics, and the settler takes his place within these structures. Managers, officials and committees exist for the smooth running of the settlement, and educational and medical services are readily available. Few people who have had the experience of living in a re-settlement area or village scheme will deny that they have profited from it. They have gained experience, self-assurance and a higher standard of living.

The relationship of the re-settlement scheme to older settlements in the same area is crucial for the future of such experiments. As long as a large proportion of the settlers is migrant and maintains a social focus in a foreign homeland, there is small chance of the new village being integrated in its immediate, rural surroundings. Integration depends on forging social relationships with the older settlements and on attracting host people to the scheme. Close social ties and intermarriage are necessarily slow in coming, but, especially in early stages of settlement, bonds are formed on the basis of immediate material needs. One basis for such relationships is the all-important question of food. Food production in East Africa is adapted very closely to particular environments that often differ widely from each other, and settlers who come from a different environment where different techniques are used, and even perhaps a different staple is grown, will find it extremely difficult to produce food for themselves and their families in the new area. Settlers may be obliged to buy food from host people, to maintain a farm for food crops in one of the traditional settlements, or even to work on a host farm for a share of the food crop.

Settlers may have other needs which can only be supplied by host people. Local shops or markets may serve the new settlement. Local craftsmen may supply settlers with tools and utensils, and, quite apart from its integration into the local administrative framework, the settlement may be fitted into other pre-existing structures—religious, legal, and so on. Many factors are involved in the process of grafting these new organs of development on to the rural social body successfully. Without careful handling and planning, rural society can form its own anti-bodies and reject the foreign tissue, causing it to wither and die.

A less violent, yet in many ways more ambitious, undertaking is the attempt to reorganize peasant farmers in their own homeland and from within their own social structures. In East Africa, co-operation is an obvious pre-condition for rural development. In Tanzania, the experiment is being made of attracting farmers to co-operate in large, communal or block farms, and the process is promoted and described in terms of the reigning political ideology of *ujamaa* (familyhood). The *ujamaa* village is a settlement in which a stricter and more thoroughgoing communalism is practised than in even the traditional village. Villagers unite on their own initiative, working together on common projects, sharing their profits equally among all those who give their labour, acquiring common facilities and setting up their own structures. The government, anxious to promote this form of co-operation is prepared to make grants of money and equipment and to offer other privileges to farmers who unite in what appears to be a serious and viable *ujamaa* scheme. Although the move is essentially voluntary, a certain amount of moral pressure and persuasion is employed, especial impetus having been given in 1971 when the best part of a million peasants joined *ujamaa* villages.

The basic obstacle to overcome in setting up the *ujamaa* village is that of mutual suspicion and the spirit of individual competition. If villagers can attain the required degree of mutual trust in one another to be equally conscientious in giving their labour and in sharing the product of that labour with others, then there is a foundation for a successful *ujamaa* village. However, a very great deal depends on the quality of leadership in the village and on relations with those who hesitate or refuse to join the experiment. It is obvious that if the leaders do not have the necessary knowledge or experience, those who participate in the *ujamaa* scheme stand to lose much more than in the case of a scheme based on individual competition. If the experiment is a failure a great many people will be affected. With proper leadership and expertise the *ujamaa* block farm should be much more effective than individual peasant enterprise.

The introduction of *ujamaa* farms in Tanzania has produced a situation comparable to that of the 1920s in Tanzania when the British Colonial Administration was seeking out the authentic rulers with a view to incorporating them into a system of so-called 'Indirect Rule'. A great many adventurers with doubtful qualifications presented themselves as authentic, traditional rulers, and contrived to get themselves accepted by the British who (as has been seen in Chapter 5) had a preconceived idea of 'chief' which they imposed on the traditional societies they ruled. Similarly, enterprising or frustrated men in the present situation have seized the opportunity provided by rural re-organization, and have offered to start an *ujamaa* village, thus securing government favour and assistance, and deploying a newly acquired power and influence. Much depends on how this power is used. If the new, *ujamaa* village is clearly delineated from existing settlements then it may well exercise a considerable power of attraction. On the other hand, if it is competing with existing settlements for local resources and amenities, particularly if it is denying these resources and amenities to existing settlements or to peasants who have traditionally enjoyed them, then the experiment may incur considerable odium. If the *ujamaa* idea is to catch on, it must not appear to penalize those who are not yet ready to become *wajamaa*.[3] It is too early to predict the future of the *ujamaa* village or to plot its relative success or failure. A rough impression is that in those areas where conditions are hard,

63

where the population is sufficiently stable and where much is to be gained from more intense co-operation, *ujamaa* is a popular idea. In fertile areas where peasants have already achieved a good deal through individual competition, the *ujamaa* idea is less attractive. Peoples with a strong hunting-gathering tradition are also hard to concentrate and it is frequently difficult to introduce the *ujamaa* idea into an already flourishing villagization scheme.

Apart from such revolutionary experiments as villagization and *ujamaa*, the only other course of action is to leave the farmer where he is and to hope to better his techniques and standard of living through a closer and more efficient training and supervision. Agricultural departments have, for a considerable time, promoted the growing of cash crops by individual peasant farmers, offering them various inducements such as credit, implements, fertilizers, and providing the seed and the produce marketing facilities. Government agricultural policy has at many times and in many places run into opposition from countrymen, tenaciously clinging to unproductive or wasteful methods bequeathed to them by tradition. It would be far too optimistic to say that this kind of opposition has been overcome, but it has certainly been lessened by public instruction and experiment. Schools and courses for farmers have been set up and there are even widely-read farmer's newspapers. Co-operatives, too, both government and non-government, have also had widespread influence, insisting, as they have done, on certain standards as a condition of membership. The result has been that the average farmer in East Africa is now much more ready to diversify and to experiment, even if he has a continual and unequal struggle against unfavourable conditions.

A recent development, especially in Kenya and Tanzania, has been the encouragement of self-help within the local community. In response to the challenges issued by governments, self-help projects, or *Harambee* projects, as they are called in Kenya, have been started in villages up and down the country. It might be the building of a school or dispensary, the making of a road or the piping of water to the village, or again, it might be the working of a communal farm or plot. In material terms, perhaps, such self-help schemes achieve little, but socially they should not be underestimated. They offer new scope for leadership and community action and they create a new mentality prepared for innovation and initiative.

In the last analysis, probably the most important factor contributing to the rural revolution, has been a steadily closer administration. 'Indirect Rule' was in many ways the symptom of an undeveloped administration. As local administration became more efficient and services to the rural areas were multiplied, there was less need to rely on traditional rulers and traditional political structures. By and large, national independence brought about a complete emancipation from them. Although there was some continuity of personnel, there was also considerable mobility. Judiciary and executive were separated; schools exerted an increasing influence; police and game department—not to mention the department of agriculture—took effective control. Above all, there appeared the focal institution of the political party, with its branches, its committees, officials and ceremonial, awakening a national consciousness in the countryside for the first time.

Finally, and as part of the closer administration just mentioned, comes the important factor of communications. The rural revolution is in part a product of improved communications—roads, railways, even airports and landing-strips, as well as postal and telegraphic services. Local problems, such as famine, epidemics among livestock, dearth of agricultural supplies, are now promptly dealt with. The transistor radio, too, exerts an influence in spreading rural development ideals. Taken all in all, the 1960s and early 1970s have probably witnessed the greatest material and social changes in the lives of rural dwelling East Africans.

8

Marriage and family life

There is no doubt at all that the traditional patterns of marriage and family life in East Africa are being radically changed at the present moment. The changes are not all even, nor are the starting points for the changes necessarily similar, since there was a variety of different family systems, in which one or another aspect of family or married life received emphasis rather than another. The transformation that is taking place is recognized, at least to the extent of idealizing the old system, and people—not necessarily old people—constantly refer to 'customary marriage' or to family 'custom' as though these things were recognizably intact at the present time. At the very least they envisage them as a kind of moral imperative, against which they judge modern developments as dangerous deviations.

Behind these attitudes lies a failure to face the facts—a failure to discern new systems and structures that are emerging and a failure to see how traditional societies, in their present rapid development, are catering, each in its own way, for new trends and forms of behaviour. It is altogether unrealistic to state the conflict in terms of African traditional marriage and family systems versus those of the western world. Easy though it may be to describe the differences in emphasis between the African family-community and the western nuclear type of family, there is no clear-cut pitched battle between the two. It is important not to see the new structures that are emerging as 'deviations' or 'adaptations' of a system, either indigenous or foreign, but rather as systems in their own right, developing rapidly it is true, but already possessing recognizable features and regularities.

Having said this, it still remains necessary to plot the changes and account for the different kinds of development that have taken place.

This inevitably means a description of 'traditional' or 'customary' marriage and family life, even if these things no longer exist in the way they are described. In East Africa, as in other parts of Africa, the family group is seen as logically prior to the institution of marriage. Whether the accent is placed on the family as a descent group, continuing its existence through the birth of successive generations, or upon the alliance which takes place between family groups through marriage, the family is seen, nevertheless, as a pre-existing entity. Traditionally in East Africa the family was a community, the basic community of society. This did not mean that it was necessarily corporate and residential, but it did usually imply that a fairly large number of kinsmen, tracing descent from a common ancestor, co-operated in various ways and exercised a certain amount of mutual co-responsibility in family affairs, particularly in such matters as inheritance, marriage and the education of children. The actual patterns of residence were more or less affected by ties of kinship, though in practice the smallest residential unit, the household, represented only a segment of the family-community. Beyond the family-community lay the wider circle of allegiance, known as the clan. Clan loyalties, names, totems and taboos were inherited through the family, and it was assumed, even if in most cases it could not be proved, that ties of consanguinity linked all the members of a particular clan category. At any rate, the rule of exogamy, or marrying outside the group, was usually rigorously applied to the category represented by the clan.

East Africa was basically patrilineal, that is to say, people inherited property and status through their father's line and belonged to their father's family community. Matriliny, in which property and status were inherited through the mother's line, was relatively rare. In point of fact, it was restricted to a group of peoples in eastern and south-eastern Tanzania. These peoples have been subjected, because of their geographical position, to an external influence that was at once earlier and stronger than in other places and the matrilineal system has deteriorated.[1] This is especially true of the Zaramo and Sagara peoples among whom the rights of fathers have triumphed over those of mother's brothers to such an extent that observers have sometimes wrongly assumed the tribes to be traditionally patrilineal. As Dr Mary Douglas has shown, matrilineal systems have a weak authority structure and encourage open recruitment for leadership when new social and economic opportunities are presented

67

to them.[2] Such has been observed among matrilineal societies in Western and even Central Africa. Without such challenges, and under pressure from the movement of patrilineals, the matrilineal structure may give way. This seems to have happened in eastern Tanzania which, from the early nineteenth century onwards, became a point of convergence for the patrilineal traders and porters of the west. It has already been noted (in Chapter 3) that eastern Tanzania was a dispersal area as early as the eighteenth century, and it does not appear that the dynastic groups which originated there were assiduous in transmitting or preserving their matrilineal institutions. Indeed, traditions suggest that these groups were themselves patrilineal. It looks, therefore, as if the disintegration of the eastern matrilineal peoples has a long history.

The matrilineal institutions of the western chieftain societies have also been noted (in Chapter 5). These have by and large, succumbed to the fissiparous tendencies of ruling dynasties and the competition between chief's sons for the high stakes represented by the ivory trade and long distance porterage to the coast. In these cases, matriliny was seldom replaced by a thoroughgoing patriliny; more often there was a total lack of any kind of system and succession to office became a matter of expediency or the work of competing pressure groups. Although matrilineal 'pockets' are occasionally found in East Africa, and institutions which often accompany matriliny, such as female initiation, bride-service or cross-cousin marriage, survive in some places, matriliny as an integrated family system has ceased to exist for a long time. This fact has contributed to the complexity of the present situation.

By contrast, patrilineal systems have stood a fairer chance of survival, and in some places, notably among the conservative pastoral societies already described (in Chapter 4), have survived pretty well intact. These, however, are the exceptions, for even if patrilineal institutions have been longer lived than their matrilineal counterparts, the bonds of patrilineal social organization have been perceptibly loosened. Patriliny remains, however, the ultimate backcloth against which the new developments are being enacted.

The family community, and particularly the patrilineal family community, was supported by a network of interacting institutions. Incest prohibitions affecting not only primary kin but a relatively large number of fairly distant kinsfolk undoubtedly buttressed the exogamic principle which obliged family communities to form alliances with each other, while retaining their distinct identities. Classificatory terminologies and forms of group reference, as well as other practices, such as the terminological merging of alternate generations, were all expressions of family solidarity in terms of age, line and generation. Bridewealth payments had important social, economic, legal and even religious connotations. Above all they were expressions of community interest in a marriage, many individuals in both the family communities involved contributing, as it were, to a family investment, in livestock or potential childbearing members of the family. Marriages were usually arranged by parents and older relatives and the rigid separation of the sexes after puberty was a safeguard for pre-marital virginity which was usually highly esteemed. Even where the having of a sweetheart was encouraged or tolerated among young people, pre-marital pregnancies were often discouraged by fierce social sanctions. Relations between the sexes were, therefore, strictly controlled by family authorities, in the interests of the family-community itself. Although the marriage contract was processual, and the process could be interrupted in its early stages on the mutual agreement of the family-communities involved, divorce properly so-called was comparatively rare.

Polygamy served the family-community by providing a larger progeny, and a larger work force for cultivation and domestic tasks. Its incidence was extremely uneven, since it depended to a great extent upon economic factors and was, indeed, one of the more important expressions of affluence. Parenthood, and the bearing of children was an obvious priority in communities struggling for survival, but polygamy catered for the barren woman, and, indeed, for widows (through the customs of levirate and widow inheritance) at a time when the single or independent woman had no role in society. Other legal fictions such as 'ghost marriage' or 'woman marriage' could save a family threatened with extinction and enable children to be born legally into it when there was no adult male to sire them. Finally, customs such as the avoidance of affines, or the mutual disrespect shown between joking partners, gave expression to the state of ambivalence that existed between family communities newly linked by marriage or between blood-relatives (cross-cousins) belonging to different family-communities.

We must now consider the changes which have taken place and which have resulted in the appearance of new types of marriage and family structure. Probably the most important and fundamental change that has taken place has been the emancipation of the younger generation. School education, the influence of Christian missions and the climate of free competition and opportunity for material advancement that now prevails in East Africa have contributed most to this movement. More than half of the population of East Africa is under twenty and these young people belong to a different culture from that of their parents. As a rule the older, rural-dwelling generation understands little or nothing of the life and atmosphere of the modern school and can offer little in the way of support and advice to youngsters who complete their education and embark on a career. Young people in East Africa today can quickly become virtually independent of their parents and they find the restraints imposed by the traditional structures of marriage and family irksome in the extreme. The arrangement of marriages is fiercely resented and is frequently condemned as an archaism in the correspondence columns of the daily newspapers. Other traditional prescriptions and prohibitions, such as, avoidance, joking, and even the prohibition of incest with distant relatives, can nowadays be more easily disregarded, since those involved find it easy to escape the sanctions, which, in any case, have been mitigated as a result of modern standards of justice and a centralized court system.

I have already mentioned the changes affecting bridewealth in the context of pastoral societies and their new experience of a money economy. Depending on the traditional social importance of the custom, bridewealth today constitutes or does not constitute a problem for the younger generation. In many places bridewealth remains merely a token or symbol and its conversion from livestock into money is not a cause of anxiety. In some places bridewealth has been adopted where in ancient times it was unknown. This has happened where matrilineal systems have given way to patrilineal ones, and where an increase of wealth and property has made the custom more practicable than bride-service. In a few, well-publicized cases, the escalation of bridewealth is a major stumbling block, and young people find it increasingly difficult to comply with the requirements of the custom. Girls tend to favour it, however, rather than boys, because it affords a greater assurance that their husbands will stay with them. On the whole, today, bridewealth is fairly easily circumvented in the initial stages of a union, although it may be an eventual feature of most unions.

Girls and boys associate far more freely today than in the past and pre-marital pregnancies are apparently far more common. The sanctions which formerly safeguarded pre-marital virginity are no longer operative or effective in a pluralistic society. However, although the need to raise up children for the family community is no longer strongly felt, there is still among young people an idealization of sexual success and the physical aspects of sex and parenthood. Many factors today militate against the custom of polygamy. One of the most important is the earlier age of marriage for men. Polygamy can only flourish where marriage is delayed and where there is a considerable disparity in the ages of husband and wives. The custom favours the older man at the expense of the younger, and it is only the well-established and economically wealthy older man who can afford to be polygamous. Today it is relatively easy for a young man to co-habit with a girl, but economically prohibitive for him to have more than one wife simultaneously. Only in highly conservative areas or in special situations such as re-settlement in a foreign area is polygamy an economic asset. On the other hand, without the social restraints of former times, successive casual unions have become more frequent, and the situation which has been described as 'mono-polygamy' is also widespread. This is the case of a man who is married to a single 'wife' but nevertheless refuses to keep and support her if she does not accept his having another household or mistress elsewhere. This is usually the first step towards desertion or separation.[3] The availability of civil divorce today helps to strengthen the position of the woman, since a 'guilty' husband is obliged to make provision for his divorced wife.

It would be unrealistic and quite premature to predict the dissolution of the family community in East Africa, although its shape and mode of operation is being profoundly modified. As was shown in the chapter on urbanization, family solidarity is an advantage for town life. Today, in a period of mobility, of glaring disparities between salary scales and standards of living, of inequalities in educational opportunities, and of differences in political and religious allegiance, it is understandable that new factors govern the composition and working of the family community. Age, line and generation are no longer sufficient criteria to establish relationships within the family. Wealth and economic position, professional seniority and education must now be taken into account. The fission of the family community may not nowadays have to wait upon the distance of its living members from a deceased common ancestor. Geographical distance between living members and socio-economic distance may today count for more, separating one segment of a family from another, or one urban network of relatives from the remainder of the family. Standards of living count for a great deal, and those who have achieved a higher standard must sometimes fight to preserve it against the encroachments of poor relations. The family community is basically a system of mutual expectations, and it cannot exist where the expectations are all on one side.

The churches have played an important part, consciously or unconsciously, in the evolution of marriage and family life in East Africa. Although they were educating the youth away from the older generations, they were, paradoxically enough, highly dependent on the rigidity and integrity of the traditional system. Christian teaching about the morality of marriage and family life usually coincided with African traditional ideas about pre-marital virginity, large families and the disapproval of infidelity and divorce. However, Christian marriage teaching was conspicuously shallow and when the traditional family structure began to break up it was too weak to hold its Christian counterpart, in existence. By and large, Christians have inherited a highly legalistic picture of the Churches' marriage ideal. Christian marriage is seen by them as a series of impossible obligations—monogamy, indissolubility, and so forth—stemming not from the nature of human love or of the marriage covenant itself, but from the partisan adherence to a church with a set of unexplained laws and dogmas. In Tanzania a popular and revealing phrase referring to church marriage was *pingu za maisha*, 'handcuffs for life'; and a Ugandan Christian in an answer to a recent survey was speaking for many others when he said: 'People today hate church marriage.'[4] Everywhere in East Africa the Christian marriage rate (number of Church weddings per 1,000 of the church population) is decreasing rapidly, and the rate is at its lowest among the peoples of the Victoria lake shore, where the oldest and best established missions are to be found.[5] In the early days when the church population structure was abnormal, when large numbers of adults were being instructed and baptized and having their pagan marriages regularized, the Christian marriage rate was abnormally high. In some places, notably eastern Uganda, less than 10 per cent of Christians getting married have a church wedding, and of these probably the majority are regularizing a union which has already been in existence for some time.

European missionaries had no real understanding of traditional family systems in East Africa. Their marriage teaching was based on the social and cultural presuppositions of western Europe or North America, including the practice of a fairly adequate period of engagement, a greater social equality between the sexes, and the autonomy of the nuclear family (parents and their immediate children). Their demand for absolute indissolubility from the beginning of the union, for monogamy and total fidelity, coupled with their condemnation of divorce, has been a direct encouragement for trial marriages. Although the trial element was present in the processual contract that characterized African traditional marriage, the trial marriage, properly so-called, is a modern development. Young couples are daunted by the seemingly impossible demands of Church marriage and so put off a formal wedding for years, even for life.

Before political independence the churches enjoyed considerable influence over the married lives of their adherents. In church schools and church hospitals employees who gave bad example were easily dismissed. Today, when control over these institutions has largely been relinquished to government, it is more difficult for the churches to exercise this kind of power. The churches' pastoral efficiency has also suffered, since recruitment to the ministry has not kept pace with the growth of church membership and it is difficult for pastors to get around and instruct their Christians for marriage, let alone preside over church weddings. Added to these handicaps is the further impediment stemming from the demands of civil law. Church marriages must be registered, and of the already insufficient number of pastors, comparatively few are licensed to register marriages for the state.

Civil law labours under many of the handicaps that apply to church law, and, indeed, it shares virtually the same historical pedigree. Only in Tanzania since 1969 has any serious attempt been made to codify customary marriage law, to bring it up to date and to reconcile it to other existing codes. The Tanzanian Marriage Law has ended the anomaly according to which, for example, polygamy was upheld by customary law and punished by civil law, and bridewealth was demanded by customary law and yet not required by civil law. The attempt has been made to hold a balance and to allow for developments. In the case of bridewealth, for example, claims can be upheld in the courts where it has been agreed to, but it is not a legal necessity for a valid marriage. Divorce, too, has been standardized, whereas in the past there were civil, Islamic and customary procedures. In Uganda the Kalema Report recommended a rationalization of the various levels of marriage law before the end of the Obote régime, but so far it has not been implemented by the government of the Second Republic.

The picture of marriage in many parts of East Africa today is one which begins with what is commonly called 'elopement'. A boy and a girl co-habit against the wishes, perhaps without the knowledge, of their parents, or at least without having fulfilled the requirements of customary marriage, but with the grudging consent of the parents. In many cases, there have been previous casual or temporary unions. This is more common in the case of the girl who starts the process at an earlier age. The union, when it survives, is converted, probably in the majority of cases, into a customary one, and the obligations are eventually for the most part fulfilled. Very often these include some kind of fine or compensation in addition to the bridewealth. In a much smaller number of cases, the union is converted into a church marriage. In these cases social and material advantages may weigh very strongly, since a church wedding, particularly in town, is an elaborate and prestigious occasion, and the registration that goes with it may entail tax benefits or emoluments of one kind or another. Civil marriages are of comparatively little importance, as long as church weddings offer more glamour, ask a smaller fee and are available at weekends.

Parental ideals have not, so far, encouraged a limitation of family size, and for most African married people, including those belonging to the educated and salaried classes, the social and educative value of the large family is highly prized. Moreover, the family community, albeit often truncated and working with new principles of organization and co-operation, is finding scope in the changing situation for collective action and co-responsibility, even if it enjoys less direct influence in the arrangement of marriages and the preparation of young people for married life. Customs like avoidance, which emphasized the control of the family community over such matters, are being undermined. This situation may be deplored by an older generation, or by those who believe that Christian marriage teaching offers a deepening of the human experience of marriage and family life, but such people must open their eyes to the reality of the present situation. This is the pattern with which educators, lawyers, administrators, churches and social workers have to deal today in East Africa.

9

Socialization and education

In the traditional societies of East Africa children were prepared in a variety of ways for their place in the social life of the adult community.[1] At one end of the scale were the numerous occasions when formal instruction was given; at the other, the experiences and voluntary associations of childhood which were all, in some way, determined by adult expectations. Such socialization or education for social life was wholly adequate for the relatively self-sufficient ethnic groups of the past. It was also fairly comprehensive, introducing the child or youth not only to the knowledge and skills appropriate for an adult of his or her sex, but also to the deeper values and beliefs of society, and to the various levels of identity and loyalty within the community. Today the educational picture is a hundred times more complex. As a consequence of the enlargement of social scale there has been a corresponding enlargement of scale in formal education. Formal education is a national concern, and young people have to be taught the skills needed to operate the highly complex machine of a modern nation-state. The appearance of the school, offering a European type of education, has triggered a revolution in East Africa. It has brought about the most far-reaching social transformation that the area has ever known, making possible national development and political independence. But the school has brought in its train a host of unexpected social problems and conflicts. Besides the competition between the school and traditional forms of socialization, there has often been a failure on the part of the school to cater for all the different levels and facets of modern social life, and more disturbing still, it is now being asked whether the European type of school system inherited from colonial times is an adequate vehicle for promoting the new political ideologies and development programmes, and whether the school is capable of being invested with wider social functions than it has hitherto enjoyed.

In traditional society, the African child was educated by a community for membership of the community. Most ethnic groups had distinctive birth-rites, in many of which the expectations of the community towards the new-born child were acted out. In these rites, neighbours sometimes mimed the adult activities appropriate to the sex of the child, hunting in the case of a boy, sweeping and cooking in the case of a girl. Such rites were a clear manifestation of the interest of the whole community in the up-bringing of the child. Later on, the child's whole education would be group-orientated. Special emphasis would be placed on behaviour outside the home, on correct social relationships, courtesies, rights and duties. The child would be taught to obey and serve all the adults in the community, and when an adult punished a neighbour's child, such an action met more often with the approval than the resentment of the parents.

Within the family community there was a shared responsibility for the child's upbringing. At different stages in its development, the child would be placed in the hands of different relatives and not exclusively in those of its own immediate parents. Psychologically, as well as socially, this system of family education held several advantages. The child developed greater self-assurance and established a wide network of personal links. Studies have suggested that children who have received this kind of home education enjoy greater success in life than those brought up exclusively in the nuclear household.[2] The sharing of parental roles in the family community reduces psychological tension. In the patrilineal family, the father exercises jural authority, while the mother's brother shows manly parental affection. The grandparents, on the other hand, show indulgence to children when young. The child spends lengthy periods in the households of relatives other than his parents, and does not, as a consequence, experience the frustrations of emerging from his childhood freedom with people with whom he is emotionally involved. Paradoxically, such children receive more attention than if they remained at home, since their own parents can be appealed to if they are badly treated. The system seems to cater for the care of children in crisis; it may also be related to apprenticeship for the learning of special skills, one relative or another having a particular specialization attractive to a younger member of the family community.

Such a system of family education certainly caters for the different facets of social life to which the child has to be introduced. Grandparents and members of the older generation introduce young children to religious beliefs and practices and to the basic values of society. They are the principal tellers of myths and folktales and singers of songs which convey such values. The child's own parents, on the other hand introduce him or her to the duties and skills belonging to his or her sex. The child learns by doing, with very little in the way of formal instruction. Responsibility is given early, in errands outside the home, in caring for flocks and herds, collecting firewood and deputizing for parents in communal activities. The child learns through imitation, and discipline is harsh, even generating fear in the child. Rewards are few and there are few strong motives for the child to give of his best. Children in East Africa, as elsewhere, enjoy playing games in which they act out their expectations of adult life. Unfortunately many parents are not convinced of the educational value of games, and regard play activity as a waste of time.

In traditional society the child was introduced to wider responsibilities within society as a whole through progressive, formal instruction and ritual. However, values pervasive to the whole society found their echo in the education the child received in the home. In Buganda (Uganda) the supreme social value was that of the Kabaka or king, epitome of paternal authority, and the young huntsman was taught to kill animals 'in the name of the Kabaka'! In Uchagga (Tanzania) the dominant value was symbolized by Kibo (Mount Kilimanjaro), the sign of precedence within a hierarchy of relationships, which demanded that youngsters allow their seniors to pass them on the side of the mountain. Among several pastoral peoples of Kenya, a dominant symbol was that of grass, the food of cattle and sign of peace and prosperity, used in a number of domestic rituals.[3]

Many East African peoples had communitarian life-crisis rituals at puberty, or before marriage. On these occasions young people were secluded in batches for instruction and trial. They were taught about the wider loyalties to clan, chiefdom and ethnic grouping, and they were prepared for their duties as adults and parents. The initiation was often climaxed by a physical operation, usually on the organs of sex, which symbolized the changed personality of the initiant emerging into adulthood, and which in some cases was a test of courage and of the ability to sublimate pain. There were also other tests of endurance and submission. By these means the young adult was prepared for the demands that society would make upon him or her. In some cases the initiation of young people was directly linked to political loyalties and was first and foremost a sign of full citizenship within the chiefdom or tribe. The circumcision of the Gisu (Uganda) and the Kikuyu (Kenya) certainly had this connotation, as did the initiation into the royal secret society, *uwuxala*, for the Kimbu (Tanzania), or the politically controlled initiations of the Pare (Tanzania). Such tendencies were at their most explicit when young people formed an adolescent peer-group placed at the service of a chief or king, or of society as a whole. Such were the warrior grades of so many Kenya pastoralists, or the court pages of the Lake Kingdoms of Uganda.

In traditional society, specialization was limited and particular skills or traditions in, for example, hunting, medicine, drumming, blacksmithing and local crafts were taught through a master-disciple relationship. Such skills were either passed down through families to talented or interested descendants, or else a young person interested in a particular craft attached himself to an adult specialist as his servant and disciple. Eventually, he either succeeded him or set up on his own.

The school was first introduced into East Africa by Christian missionaries at the close of the nineteenth century. Its nearest precursor was the Muslim Qur'an school, but this was limited to the areas of Muslim influence at the coast. It was also rigidly circumscribed by immediate religious needs. The new Christian school, on the other hand, although it resembled the Qur'an school in that its chief purpose was religious instruction, nevertheless assumed that a humane, and even a technical, education was necessary. Christianity, it was assumed, went hand in hand with material 'civilization' and with an improvement in the quality of life of those evangelized. Christian missionaries therefore taught the 'three Rs' as well as the catechism. Everywhere 'bush-schools' were set up by the missionaries and confided to local catechists or evangelists. Training centres were also established for these catechists, which were the forerunners of the modern Teachers' Training Colleges. By the 1920s the churches had put their whole weight behind education, seeing in the school the chief instrument of evangelization and church growth.

Inevitably, the church school clashed with the institutions of traditional society. It was seen as a rival to the politically controlled initiation rites and adolescent peer-groups, and chiefs in the early days fought the school tooth and nail. Traditional rulers resented the withdrawal of the youth from their own influence, and this was certainly one of the major issues in the persecution of the neophytes in Buganda in the 1880s which culminated in the well-known martyr-doms. Gradually, however, as the developing colonial administra-tions found the local rulers they wanted and began to back the educational effort of the missionaries, opposition to the schools subsided. Education was organized centrally and the church schools and training centres were secularized, in many cases being eventually taken out of the hands of the churches altogether. From the 1920s an immense expansion in education took place. Today Kenya has more than a million children in primary schools and 89,000 in second-ary schools, three times the figure of ten years ago. Uganda has 650,000 children in primary schools and 35,000 in secondary schools, while Tanzania has 800,000 in primary schools and 28,000 in secondary schools. About half the boys and a third of the girls of primary school age are at school, and from 2 to 4 per cent of children in the 14–17 age group are at secondary school. These proportions may not look impressive, but in fact there is a great deal of dropping in and out of school and it has been reckoned that almost all boys and over half the girls get some schooling today, however minimal. There is no doubt that the school has been the principal agent of social change, responsible for the break-up of the traditional ethnic groups as political entities.

The school also represented a threat to traditional family educa-tion. It placed great emphasis on obedience and self-reliance, it is true, but it stressed intellectual achievements far more than practical skills. Frankness, honesty and trust were inculcated in the students but education was more person-orientated than group-orientated. It was more important to be a nice person in oneself than to observe courtesies and be ready to serve and obey outsiders. Private owner-ship was another value taught at school, and great importance was attached to hygiene. But above all, in the eyes of the parents and the students themselves, the school was an automatic process through which a child could acquire the necessary skills to carry out the highly paid jobs created by the administration. The school was the gateway to a new world.

Inevitably, family education suffered. A gulf was opened between

79

parents and children. On the one hand, parents knew nothing of the school and school life and were quite unable to advise their children. On the other, children tended to despise their parents. Very little formal instruction could be given to a school-child in the home, and moral formation and preparation for marriage were neglected. Unfortunately, the school did not make up for this lack of moral education, partly as the churches lost their influence over education, but more especially because school education was too bookish. Students were far too absorbed by the mechanics of preparing for, and sitting, examinations. Education became a rat race and there was little time for moral education or character formation. Even sports suffered.

Puberty rituals declined everywhere, with a few notable exceptions. Where they possessed value as a cultural symbol, or a symbol of ethnic loyalty, they survived. Examples are found among the Kikuyu in Kenya, the Gisu in Uganda, and the Yao, Makua and Makonde peoples of south-east Tanzania. Yet even here the rites were attenuated to such a degree that little has remained of them other than a somewhat unhealthy preoccupation with a physical operation on the organs of sex. The wealth of instruction and ritual that formerly accompanied the operation and gave it meaning has largely disappeared.

But it was not only the school that made its impact on traditional social and family life. Changes in family structure could also affect the school performance of the child. Marital instability and parental separation left their mark, and it has been noted that children from broken families more frequently drop out of school or miss schooling altogether, suffer from malnutrition, are obliged to stay with irresponsible people and undergo considerable cruelty. Greater permissiveness among young people often leads to early pregnancies for girls, and this is always a barrier to continuing education at school. These factors frequently lead to the alienation and frustration of young people.

As was remarked in Chapter 7, the educational system developed under the British colonial administration in East Africa was geared to produce an élite. An educational pyramid was set up with a high drop-out rate at the base. As has been noted, a very small percentage of primary school leavers reach secondary school. Out of every hundred students in Form I of secondary school, some fourteen to sixteen drop out before reaching Form IV, and from eighteen to twenty fail the School Certificate Examination. Out of the sixty-six passes, some twenty-seven go on to take the course for Higher School Certificate and only fifteen or sixteen enter university. For every 700 students in Form I, therefore, there will be 100 university graduates nine years later. What happens to all those who fall by the wayside? Are there jobs for them, and are they adequately prepared for the jobs? It must be admitted that the system of education is largely determined by the end University product. Technical and commercial schools are comparatively few and are, in fact, as élitist as the university. The student who drops out of the running is in for a difficult time. Clerical and commercial jobs just do not exist for the majority of school leavers who aspire to them. The school leaver only stands some chance if he can undergo further vocational or professional training and acquire some experience. Even then the quality of instruction in many schools is so poor that the student can hardly acquire sufficient fluency in English or competence in Mathematics to perform the jobs to which he aspires. For the vast majority of primary school leavers there is no other prospect than a return to the land.

Uganda is a country which has tolerated a large number of private secondary schools. These enable more primary school leavers to continue their education than would otherwise be the case. However, in many cases they serve merely to postpone and aggravate the ultimate frustration felt by the student. The quality of teaching is often very poor in these private schools and, what is worse, the students who attend them suffer severe privations, living in appalling conditions, working at night or during the day when they are not at school, and being subjected to demoralizing influences. Very few of them live in conditions which are conducive to preparing for an important examination, and a much higher number fail than in government secondary schools.

The history of university education in East Africa begins with Makerere Technical School in 1922. This eventually developed into the University College which was affiliated to London University in 1949. By 1963, when it became, along with University College Nairobi and University College Dar-es-Salaam, a constituent college of the 'paper' University of East Africa, Makerere had over 1,000 students. In 1970 the University of East Africa ceased to exist and the Universities of Makerere, Nairobi and Dar-es-Salaam came into being. By then, Makerere had some 2,000 students with accommodation being constructed for nearly 1,000 more. Figures at Nairobi and Dar-es-Salaam were comparable. In addition there were large numbers of students abroad, and of these Kenya, with more than 2,000, had the largest number.

The problem before the independent governments of the three countries was, on the one hand, how to make education more realistic, and on the other, how to avoid the élitist mentality. Governments wanted the schools to produce useful and responsible citizens, men and women with initiative, willing to serve their country and their local community. Service was emphasized rather than rewards, and agricultural development rather than urban, clerical employment. The difficulty has been that whatever is taught there, the school seems to influence the outlook of the students in certain determined ways. Civics may be taught, school self-help projects successfully carried out, but the cumulative impact of the school system is still to produce students who are individualistic, urban-orientated, uninterested in politics and having a low degree of civic idealism. The school system of its very nature has an academic emphasis. Academic performance is certified by examination, and success in examination is rewarded by greater responsibilities and opportunities and higher salaries. Students in the higher levels of education are suspicious of the restraints placed upon them, of educational developments dictated by short-term manpower needs, and by anything that savours of the lowering of standards.[4]

Tanzania has gone further than the other two East African countries in the attempt to make education more realistic. East Africa now has its own examination system, but Tanzania has even dissociated herself from this and created a Tanzanian one. The use of an African national language, *ki-Swahili*, in the schools has been an important factor in this decision, but equally important has been the desire to orientate students towards the needs of their own country. The Tanzanian government would like to use the school not only as an instrument of education for the students who attend it, but as an organ of progress and development in the local community. The school is to be a model of the ideal community. Such an undertaking is doubly difficult. First because the adult expectations of this kind of school are located outside the local community, and second because, as we have seen, the school system in itself encourages élitism.

Tanzania, and to a lesser extent the other countries, have tried to counteract the élitist mentality among the more highly educated youth by involving them in forms of public service. In Tanzania, National Service takes the form of para-military training for six months at a camp before the students are admitted to university. Besides weapon training, a great deal of agriculture and community development work is done. Civics occupy an important place in the training programme, and there are numerous cultural activities such as traditional dancing. The student continues his National Service at the university or training college and must work during his first years of employment at a reduced salary. How far such measures have been successful is arguable. Students are cowed but resentful of the hardships to which they are subjected, and rebelliousness and unrest at the university show that National Service has not always altered the expectations shaped by the school system.

The problem of education in East Africa will not find a solution until a school system can be created the effects of which coincide with government ideals, and until those ideals are widely shared by the adult community. Government, parents and students themselves must see eye to eye about the nature and purpose of school education, and this education itself must become more realistic and more human.

10

Religious trends

The social anthropologist is sometimes depicted as a kind of archae-ologist, digging through the topsoil of modern, westernized be-haviour down to the authentic level of unadulterated tradition. Such a picture is most frequently drawn in connection with the study of religion, and there is a popular idea that religious beliefs and practices have overlaid and obscured one another like archaeological strata. On the surface lie the imported or established religions—the various forms of Christianity and Islam, for example—while at the bottom lies all that remains of the once flourishing traditional religions. Somewhere in between lie the middle strata of the African Independent Churches, offering a mixture of elements from both upper and lower levels. It is assumed that the anthropologist must ignore the topsoil, and must interest himself only in what is original, authentic or traditional.

Such a picture is absurdly naïve. Religious systems do not simply overlay each other; on the contrary, there is a dialectic or interchange between them and they influence each other to a greater or lesser extent. Moreover, it is a mistake to imagine that the established or orthodox Churches are somehow immune to indigenous influences, and that it is only the Independent Churches which owe anything to ideas and values stemming from traditional religion. The relative success or failure of orthodox Christianity in any area depends to a large extent on pre-existing social factors. It is true, of course, that traditional beliefs and practices are apparently disappearing. They were articulated wholly within the social and political structure of the tribe. When the structure disappeared, visible religious practice disappeared also. In this process the churches were only one of the many agents at work. Yet if traditional religion today hardly enjoys any independent existence of its own, that is not the same thing as saying that traditional religious ideas and values, and even some practices, have not found a new lease of life within the new religious structures. We shall consider evidence that they have.

Traditional religion in East Africa was articulated wholly within the structure of the tribe. Its beliefs and values were taught through communitarian rituals. Worship was conducted by representatives of the different social groupings—clan, family, chiefdom, professional association. Religious beliefs represented the attempt to come to grips with a particular experience—experience of environment and way of life, experience of a particular history lived in this environment, and a particular social experience. All these factors accounted for the different combinations and emphases within the various traditional religious systems, and contributed to an original view of man and his relationship to the world which was the basis for a characteristic value system. These ideas and values were expressed in an equally characteristic form of symbolic classification.

Obviously, the study of traditional religion is ultimately inseparable from the study of traditional society as a whole. On the other hand, religious ideas and practices had a currency wider than the tribe. Elements were widely shared, although they occupied places of differing importance within particular religious systems, and their symbolism varied from one grouping to another. There was also a historic sharing of ideas which appeared first of all as responses to particular environments. These facts give a certain validity to the limited generalizations which can be made here.

Basic to the systems of religious belief in East Africa is the notion of 'spirit' or 'ultra-human power' expressed in certain generic linguistic terms. Among the speakers of the so-called Bantu languages the related terms *mungu, mulungu, murungu, mu'ungu* are nowadays applied to specific personal manifestations of spirit, for example, the ancestors or the High God himself, while the term *kilungu, kirungu* is applied to the conus-shell disc-emblem which was the symbol of the divine power of chiefs and elders. Among the Nilotic Lwoo speakers, however, it is more difficult to tie the terms *jok, juok* down to any personal manifestation. Rather, *jok* or *juok* is encountered at different levels of experience, including belief in ancestor spirits, and there is no single reality behind this multiple experience.[1] Probably, however, the majority of East African peoples had an idea of a High God who was also the Creator. The sky symbolism which is used to refer to the supreme being reflects different cosmological patterns, but on the whole it expresses the way in which the powers in general, and the creator in particular, transcend human experience and the realm of men which is the earth. Often, too, it expresses human dependence upon phenomena associated with the sky, such as rainfall, cloud and sunshine, of great importance to cultivators in an uncertain climate. A very common sky symbol applied to the High God in East Africa is that of the sun.[2] This symbol unites a chain of peoples stretching from south-western Tanzania to the north-east, and across the Kenya border, Kimbu, Pimbwe, Nyamwezi, Iramba, Issanzu, Gogo, Kuria, Sonjo, Chagga, Pare and Mbugwe. In the south-east and across the border into Central Africa, the symbol of lightning, or the thunder-bolt, represented by the term *lesa, ileesa, leza*, unites another group of peoples, while the less specific symbol of 'sky' typifies the pastoral peoples, like the Karimojong of north-eastern Uganda for whom the word is *akuj*.

Creation signifies the epitome of ownership and control, even if it is not strictly creation *ex nihilo*. A very large number of East African peoples, especially in western Tanzania and western Uganda, have specific and related terms meaning 'creator', *matunda, umatunda, katonda*. Moreover, creation is often conceived on an analogy with human fatherhood and begetting. The creator is essentially a life-giver, the ultimate origin of life and of the conditions of life. Myths of creation abound, and so also do myths which suggest that the human abuse of created things meets with punishment. One recurring example is that of the hunter or trapper who was too successful and who was finally hunted down by the herds and flocks he had decimated.

Nature Spirits correspond to the human experience of an unfamiliar or potentially hostile world. In some cases these are personalized experiences not defined by a worshipful attitude or by any spirit of dependence through prayer or sacrifice. At other times, they are very clearly the objects of religious activity. One of the most important figures is the Master of the Animals or the Great Herder, a spirit which, among hunting-gathering peoples, is identified with the supreme being himself, but which, among peoples for whom hunting is a specialization, becomes a largely unfriendly and quixotic being. Once again there are numerous myths of salvation from the clutches of this being or beings, found in the oral literature of nearly every East African ethnic group.[3]

Since the majority of East African peoples are settled cultivators, having the graves of their dead in or near their settlements, one would expect a cult of lineage or ancestor spirits. In many religious systems ancestor spirits appear to occupy the most prominent position. Such spirits not only offer a *rationale* for social groupings such as family, clan, chiefdom or specialist association, but they betoken an esteem for the personal worth of human beings who live in the human memory and who symbolize important social values such as authority, fecundity, social influence, material success and so forth. Ancestors are venerated not merely by explicit acts of worship, offerings at shrines and so on, but by the naming of children and by invocation in blessings. They are closely linked to prevailing moral ideals which are not necessarily strictly ethical. Nevertheless, the idea that certain human faults not only threaten other human beings, but even offend the spiritual powers is certainly present, and there are widespread rituals of purification which symbolize either a spiritual washing or cleansing, or else getting rid of a state of enmity or danger. Monica Wilson has described very fully the purificatory rites which typify Nyakyusa traditional religion in southern Tanzania.[4]

Finally, geography and economics have their religious aspect. Sacred places and mythical places of origin contribute to a kind of mystical geography, extending far beyond the borders of a particular ethnic grouping. Mountains and hills are obvious symbols of sublimity and transcendence, comparable to the importance of sky symbolism, and mounts Kenya and Kilimanjaro play an expected role in the religious symbolism of the peoples who live near them. Other mountains, for example Mount Hanang in Tanzania, are associated with rain-making and the source of rain. Such geographical features figure in a great many traditions of migration and myths of origin. The social importance of cattle among pastoral peoples has been noted in an earlier chapter, and it is therefore understandable that cattle should have a religious value. For pastoralists, the goings and comings of the herds between kraal and grazing grounds, may symbolize, as among the Gogo of Tanzania, the bridge provided by religious practices between the world of spirits and the world of men.[5] Even more directly, cattle constitute such a link in themselves when they are sacrificed.

The penetration of East Africa by Christian missionaries began in the mid-nineteenth century, with the freed slave settlements of the

Anglican Church Missionary Society and the Roman Catholic Holy Ghost Fathers along the coast of what is now the Tanzanian mainland. By 1890 the Church Missionary Society and Universities Mission to Central Africa (Anglican) had pushed north-west to Uganda and south-west to Lake Nyasa respectively, while the London Missionary Society (Congregationalist) and United Methodist Mission were established respectively in central Tanzania and south-eastern Kenya. At the same time the Roman Catholic White Fathers had begun to infiltrate the whole region of the Great Lakes. In the next two decades the Bethel, Berlin and Leipzig Lutherans had established themselves in northern and southern Tanzania, and the Moravians from Herrnhüt had occupied the missions of the departed London Missionary Society in the west of the country. The Benedictines (Roman Catholic) were occupying eastern Tanzania and the Roman Catholic Mill Hill Fathers from London had partitioned Uganda with the White Fathers and were settling in western Kenya. In addition, the Holy Ghost Fathers and the Seventh Day Adventists had entered Kenya and northern Tanzania, and the Church of Scotland, Church of God, Quakers and Protestant African Inland Mission were also in Kenya. In the early years of the twentieth century the Roman Catholic Consolata Fathers began to evangelize the Kenya Highlands, and at the same time another Italian missionary order, the Verona Fathers, entered northern Uganda from the Sudan. After the Second World War, East Africa experienced a further spate of missionary endeavour, with more Protestant Churches (chiefly from America) and more Roman Catholic missionary orders setting up missions.

Little more than a century after the birth of Islam, Muslims brought their religion to the East African coast from Arabia and Persia.[6] Although it merged successfully with Bantu traditions, finding an essential parallelism with them and creating the coastal Swahili culture, Islam never expanded beyond the confines of these communities which looked to the sea rather than to the unknown interior of the mainland. During the nineteenth century some coastal tribes of Kenya and Tanzania became Swahili-ized, and experienced a measure of Islamization. The slave trade, although it brought about a few incidental conversions in the interior, was largely a barrier to effective Islamization. It was noticeable that as soon as the trade was suppressed Islam enjoyed a much greater success in the coastal regions. Profiting by the relative peace and security which was a consequence of colonization, Islam began to spread inland along the trade routes. The building of the railways before the First World War gave an immense impetus to this movement and Muslim traders set up their small businesses in the towns and in the vicinity of the railway. Another important factor in the spread of Islam was the growth of migrant labour from the interior to the coastal plantations. Here the migrants fell under Swahili and Islamic influence and brought these influences back to their home areas. Colonial officials also looked with approval upon Islam as a foil for the too powerful Christian missionaries, and Muslims were sometimes favoured for positions in the local administration. This fact explains why so many chiefly families converted to Islam. Groups of Sudanese Muslims, known misleadingly as 'Nubians' (from the Nuba Mountains, not Nubia) have also settled in various parts of East Africa, remaining unassimilated, while Galla and Somali Muslims from Ethiopia and Somalia have entered northern Kenya. Although East African Islam is basically Arabian and Shafi'i, Shi'ite sects from India and Pakistan, as well as the syncretist Ahmaddiya (also from the Indian sub-continent) have established themselves in the three countries.

Early Christian efforts were concentrated on the freed slave villages with little or no attempt to make any impact on the traditional social structures. Uganda was the exception. Here the explorer H. M. Stanley had drawn attention to the impressive organization and development of the kingdom of Buganda and had invited missionaries to make of its ruler 'a Christian Prince'. Protestants and Catholics alike entered Buganda with the ultimate intention of setting up a Christian kingdom. They had reckoned, however, without the *Kabaka* (king) Mutesa I, whose political interest it was to keep the mutually intolerant missionaries prisoners at his court and to play them off against each other. Ultimately, however, the missions were too powerful for the African ruler, and the persecution of Christians ordered by Mutesa's weak successor, Mwanga, could not prevent the formation of powerful warring Christian factions. The British colonial administration encouraged the creation of separate religious spheres, and a careful distribution of offices between the denominations was made, thereby rendering the religious parties even more rigid and intolerant of each other. Proselytism throughout Uganda consisted of a race for the chiefs, it being assumed that a key convert would encourage mass conversions in a highly centralized and authoritarian society. This hope was largely fulfilled, for kings and chiefs in their turn were often on the look-out for a religion that would give them ascendancy over the rival clan cults. Several consequences have followed. Uganda is massively Christian, nearly half of the total population belonging to one of the Christian churches. African church leadership has come early—the first African Roman Catholic Bishop of modern times came from Buganda. And although Christianity has been accepted for its very foreignness, complete with all its cultural non-essentials, church structures have been strongly influenced by—and have, indeed, blended easily with—traditional authoritarianism. Dioceses correspond with the ethnic boundaries, and there is more than a grain of truth in the assertion that the Christian bishops have stepped into the shoes of the deposed kings and chiefs.

In other parts of East Africa, Christian missionaries had the same kind of success (if success it can be called) in the centralized, unitary societies.[7] Uchagga and Buhaya are examples in Tanzania. In the unitary societies which were stratified rather than centralized there was no chance of finding a key convert who would influence others. This was the case of the Kikuyu, the Masai, the Nandi and many other peoples, mainly in Kenya. Similarly, among the Luo (Lwoo) of Kenya and northern Tanzania who were divided into small households with virtually no intermediary vertical units, orthodox Christianity made little headway. It was either rejected altogether or it was radically adapted to their way of life by the people themselves. Both the Luo and the Kikuyu areas are centres of independent church movements.

In the pluralistic context of the multi-chiefdom societies which characterize probably the greater part of Tanzania, the Christian churches have found themselves competing with each other and with traditional religious associations and allegiances. They have all too easily fitted into the pre-existing pluralistic pattern, and have often been forced into a marginal role. In areas of migration and re-settlement, however, Christianity has achieved success, offering security and identity to immigrant groups. Christianity has served quite often as a vehicle of protest against tradition, as a means of escaping unpleasant social obligations and of achieving a new status through school education.

Protestant churches, like those founded by the Church Missionary Society or the Moravian Brothers have managed to operate with limited expatriate personnel, and they have Africanized easily.

Roman Catholics, on the other hand, have laboured under the disadvantage that a sacramental church requires a large body of ministers. Added to this has been the requirement of a high standard of education for the local clergy. These factors have combined to ensure a slow build-up of local clergy and a high drop-out rate from the seminaries. While the church population is steadily growing, the proportion of clergy to Christians is becoming more and more unfavourable, and there is an increasing dependence upon lay catechists, teachers and sisters to whom sacramental functions are being given. With mounting governmental pressure on the expatriates to depart, the proportion of expatriate to local clergy is becoming more and more anachronistic. In Uganda the local clergy are 37 per cent of the total, while in Tanzania they are 32 per cent. In Kenya, however, they are a mere 12 per cent. African sisterhoods, on the other hand, have had a much greater numerical success. In Uganda Africans are 77 per cent of the sisters: in Tanzania, 63 per cent and in Kenya 41 per cent. It is clear that Roman Catholics will have to restructure their ministry, if they are to cater for the needs of their Christians.

Orthodox or mission, Christianity in East Africa is strictly tied financially and organizationally to the 'white' mother churches of the western world. However, Roman Catholics and Anglo-Catholics—particularly in the pluralistic societies of Tanzania—have been able to go some way towards Africanizing their catechesis and ritual. The earliest attempt was made by the Anglo-Catholic Bishop Lucas at Masasi (Tanzania) in 1919 and consisted in the adaptation of local initiation rites.[8] The experiment, which was later copied by Roman Catholics, was largely unsuccessful because it impoverished the traditional symbolism, weakened social bonds and was not organically linked to the sacramental system of the church itself. However, not only have the churches begun to appreciate the value of African traditional religion more and more, but a theological revolution has taken place which allows them to take a far more positive attitude towards non-Christian religions. The Protestant churches, by and large, have been less affected by this trend than those which belong to the Catholic tradition. It is one thing, however, to ask, 'How African is Christianity in East Africa?' Another important question is, 'How Christian is Christianity in East Africa?' Adaptation is not necessarily a conscious process, and there are signs that African Christians care less for the more specifically Christian dog-

91

mas than for those aspects of Christianity which reinforce and develop their traditional idea of God and their traditional morality. The question is, 'How central is the person of Christ to the beliefs and practices of Christians in East Africa?' It is a fact that many Christians continue to indulge in traditional practices which either conflict with official Christianity, or with which official Christianity has not yet come to terms.

Muslims, who count some 10 per cent of the total East African population (as opposed to the Christian proportion of 37 per cent), have not only *not* experienced a noticeable conflict with African religious tradition, but have been accused of capitulating to it. Certainly, the social aspect of Islam has been more important to its adherents than its dogmas. Controversies and secessions have taken place as a result of disputes about the conduct of prayer and the use of drums, and the most popular practice has been the recitals of *mawulids* (*maulidi*) in honour of the prophet Mohammed at social gatherings. Unfortunately, Islam has lagged behind the Christian churches in promoting education and in acquiring a position of influence in the country. Uganda, which has the smallest percentage of Muslims of any East African country, now possesses a government with a Muslim president, Muslim interests, and favouring alliances with Muslim countries. Attempts are being made to redress the balance by setting up Islamic institutions of learning in Uganda, and Ugandan Muslims have found an unaccustomed unity in the Muslim Supreme Council which the government has imposed upon them.

Finally, we must take a look at a very important religious development, that of the African independent churches. Although Kenya is, perhaps, the country most affected by the movement of independency, all three countries have experienced it. Following Harold Turner's classification, these movements are of three main types:[9] Christian churches which have seceded from white mission churches, like the secession of the African Greek Orthodox Church from the Anglican Church of Uganda or the Legio Maria Church from the Roman Catholic Church in Kenya; Hebraist, or 'Old Testament' churches, like the African-Israel-Church-in-Nineveh also in Kenya; and neo-pagan movements which are new forms of the traditional religion like the Maji Maji movement in the first decade of the twentieth century in Tanzania. We have already noted that certain types of traditional social organization favoured the growth of independent churches rather than the acceptance of mission Christianity.

There were a number of other reasons which encouraged independency. As Welbourn has pointed out, Christianity in its mission form was not radically united to the rational structures of African society, particularly in the types of society already referred to.[10] Moreover, that society appeared to be threatened by modern changes. Independent church movements partly transposed the social problem on to a mythical plane, helping the African 'to feel at home' in the changed situation, and partly helped to rebuild his society, especially his experience of the local community. These tendencies were reflected in the particularism, and even the tribalism, of some independent churches, and also in the preoccupation with healing from a complex of sickness, witchcraft and moral evil. Barrett has identified as principal religious cause an insensitivity for African social institutions on the part of the mission churches—'an unconscious failure in love'—causing a resentment that surfaced on the occasion of some trivial dispute, a flashpoint that ended in secession. Independency was one way of being African in a colonial world dominated by Europeans and, for this reason, these church movements contributed greatly to the rise of nationalism and African political consciousness. Maji Maji was a revolt against the Germans in Tanzania. Elijah Masinde, with his Religion of the Ancestors (*Dini ya Misambwa*) in Kenya, had to be pacified by a colonial army. The independent Kikuyu churches of Kenya played an important role in the Mau Mau campaign and in the challenge to the colonial administration. Even Reuben Spartas's secession from the Church of Uganda to form the African Greek Orthodox Church was associated with the riots that took place from 1948 to 1950.

As I said at the beginning of this chapter, it is unrealistic to see religions as levels or layers, superimposed on each other. It is equally wrong to see them purely in conflict and competition. In fact, there is a great deal of mutual aid, mutual influence and borrowing. The different religions cater for different social and religious needs, and, in many ways, complement each other. Orthodox, or mission, Christianity has been slow to make a successful synthesis of Christian and African religious traditions. The independent churches have made the synthesis at a less sophisticated level. The chances are that both will grow nearer and more similar to each other, the mission churches becoming more African in character and the independent churches becoming more orthodox and more sophisticated.

II

Spirit possession and communities of affliction

Spirit possession or spirit mediumship was fairly common among the traditional religious systems of East Africa.[1] There are signs today of a development—even an increase—in these practices. That this is related to the experience of widespread change seems undeniable. Beattie has noted the function of spirit possession to comprehend and incorporate change and Turner has introduced us to the concept of the 'liminal' ritual which is a prolongation of the liminal phase in a *rite de passage*, through which individuals find strength to meet the demands of a complex and highly structured society.[2] Liminal rituals characterize liminal periods of history when an old social order is passing away and a new one has not yet clearly taken shape. Turner has also described the 'community of affliction' whereby a group of individuals come to terms with an affliction or a sickness as a group,[3] and Mary Douglas has shown how the physical body, its sufferings and pains, must be correlated to the categories in which society is seen.[4] The growing preoccupation with rituals to cure bodily ills reflects the sickness of the old social order and the unconscious desire to repair it.

Basically, spirit possession can only be defined as the belief of members of a certain society that people are possessed by a spirit or spirits. Usually, however, it is a real or assumed trance that constitutes the evidence of possession, and the actions of the person in this state which are interpreted as evidence of control by a spirit normally external to him. The term 'spirit mediumship' is used to refer to the idea of a possessed person serving as an intermediary between spirits and human beings. In such cases the language or actions of the medium have to be translated. Obviously belief in spirit possession depends, in turn, upon belief in a spirit world peopled with various spirit forces with which human beings can communicate through mediumship. However, there are many different kinds of spirit. Some of these spirits are clearly the objects of a religious or worshipful attitude, in which case mediumship is a more direct method of contact with them than sacrifice or prayer. At the other end of the spectrum are many non-religious spirits—personifications of experiences, causes of illnesses and so forth. These are kinds of talking germs, viruses or psychic forces, or they may resemble the 'fairies' and the 'leprechauns' of Irish rural tradition. Whether or not they are objects of a religious cult, all spirits are malevolent some of the time, and their hostility may be justified as a punishment for human neglect or wrong-doing.

The purpose of spirit possession and the rituals connected with it may be divinatory—to discover hidden events or hidden causes of misfortune. Or the purpose may be frankly religious—to honour and appease the spirit and invite his protection. Or else the aim is to remove an affliction or misfortune by persuading the spirits to depart or to keep their distance. Often, it is believed, the solution can be found by establishing a harmonious relationship with the spirits. Frequently, too, the idea of a community or guild enters in and possession is part of a long and elaborate initiation, with regular celebrations. Many techniques are used to induce the state of mental dissociation or trance. In some cases it is a question of singing, drumming and shaking rattles; in others, inhalants such as vapours from a steaming pot of medicine or incense smoke are employed; at other times incisions are made in the initiant's body and medicine is rubbed in, or else the patient is made to drink a medicine which is a decoction of leaves and roots. In very many cases the process begins with the diagnosis of a patient's illness as spirit activity. As a result of the rituals and trances the patient may or may not recover. Usually however, recovery is a slow process and the sufferer has a constant need to return to the rituals and for communication with the spirits. This need reinforces the institutional character of spirit possession and there are frequently successive grades or steps in the spirit possession guild to which the sufferer belongs. Many of the spirit illnesses are symptoms of nervous states accompanying a diminution or lack of status. These are more easily cured. However, spirit possession guilds can even help their members to accept incurable conditions.

We have already noted that spirit possession was a feature of traditional religious sytems in East Africa, but that there have been widespread developments of the phenomenon to help people come to terms with social change. Lewis has made a distinction between spirit possession cults which are 'central' and those which are 'peripheral'.[5] The central cult is one which is central to the maintenance of morality in society, either as a divinatory method of identifying anti-social elements, such as witches and sorcerers, or as a means of strengthening solidarity between living human beings on the one hand and lineage or territorial spirits on the other. The peripheral cult refers, not to traditional institutions and values, but rather to contact between different cultural traditions, reactions to a changing environment and to what Southall calls 'psycho-cultural threats.'[6]

It would be wrong to describe the adepts of spirit possession in East Africa as deviant or deprived people. Psychological hypotheses are not an adequate explanation of the phenomenon. Moreover, particularly in the case of central cults, spirit mediums are highly respected people and pillars of a traditional value system. However, it is true to say that mediums are often chosen because of their liminal character. They are very often older women or young, 'innocent' people, or they may be men who are impotent, homosexuals or transvestites. In the case of peripheral cults, spirit possession caters for persons of low social status and for those whose status is uncertain or threatened by social change. The guild creates its own symbolical and mythological world, and escape into this world confers status because its very strangeness commands fascination and respect.

One important aspect of spirit possession is its dramatic character. This is obviously enhanced when mental dissociation is simulated, rather than real, but all spirit possession has a theatrical quality. The medium impersonates a spirit, acting out a particular role and speaking, or purporting to speak, a language which suits the role. In a similar way early Egyptian and Greek drama, ancestors of the modern western theatre, consisted in players impersonating the gods and enacting the myths concerning them. In East Africa, increased mobility and the improvement in communications have enlarged the *dramatis personae* of the spirit possession guilds, new ideas and new characters being continually adopted. Many of the new characters are borrowed from Christian theology or from the European way of life to which frustrated people aspire.

Before examining examples of both central and peripheral spirit possession in East Africa, we must refer again to the chain of traditions about the Chwezi (Cwezi, Swezi) which, as we noted in the chapter on chieftain societies, unites so many different people in western Uganda and western Tanzania.[7] These traditions stretch from West Nile in Uganda where the Alur represent the northern-most margins of the Chwezi complex, down to the Kimbu in south-western Tanzania who represent the southernmost limits of Chwezi influence. The Chwezi myths occupy positions of varying importance in the cultures of the different ethnic groups. In Bunyoro and Ankole (Uganda) the Chwezi are hero-gods, and possession by the Chwezi spirits is a central cult with the social function of articulating the lineages within a centralized political order, and sanctioning tradi-tional beliefs and institutions. In Alur (Uganda) and Usukuma (northern Tanzania) the Chwezi cults have no direct connection with the mythology of Bunyoro and Ankole, but in Unyamwezi (central Tanzania) the Buswezi cult has inherited the myths and songs of the lake kingdoms via the central possession cults of Rwanda, Burundi and Buha (western Tanzania). In southern Unyamwezi and in Ukimbu (southern Tanzania) the Chwezi songs have been appropri-ated by the *migawo* cult which is centred on an altogether different mythology. The songs are not understood and have merely been borrowed because they are attractive and musically superior to the other songs available. In all the cultures but that of the lake king-doms spirit possession is largely peripheral and constitutes an attempt to comprehend and incorporate change, although the power and the prestige of the Buswezi cult in Unyamwezi has exercised an attraction for the traditional rulers who have tried to align themselves with it and even control it. Social and psychosomatic therapy are important subsidiary functions, as is sheer entertainment.

In Bunyoro and Ankole each agnatic group is associated with a Chwezi hero spirit known as *mbandwa/emandwa*.[8] This spirit looks after the well-being, health and prosperity of the homestead and has his own medium who is initiated into his service. In Bunyoro there are also 'black *mbandwa*', as opposed to these 'white *mbandwa*' who protect the household. The black *mbandwa* is thought to be mainly malevolent and represents forces that originate outside Bunyoro. *Ndege* is the spirit of aeroplanes; *njungu*, the spirit of Europeanness; *kifaru*, the spirit of military tanks and so on. Such spirits represent the reaction to foreign contact and are decidedly peripheral. In

97

Ankole, however, the attempt is being made in some areas to assimilate the new forces to the central possession cult. A syncretist movement has grown up known as Bachwezi.[9] The adepts of this movement are Christians who, in imitation of the Roman Catholic association the Legion of Mary, place a small stool or table in their houses with a table-cloth, flowers and religious objects on it. This stool or table is the seat of a *mucwezi* who is identified as the Virgin Mary, or one of the saints or angels, and who is regarded as a protector-spirit of the household. A member of the household becomes a medium for this spirit who reveals to him the secrets of certain medicines and remedies. The initiant can, in turn, initiate others and exorbitant fees are charged for this service. It would appear that trance is mostly simulated in this cult.

In north-western Uganda, Southall found the same syncretism and use of a Christian altar.[10] The *jok* concept of the Alur embraces all spirit phenomena and is thus able to accommodate spirit personalities from neighbouring Bantu peoples and from missionary religions. Jok Hala represents the muslim deity Allah, for example, in one of the cults. Besides catering peripherally for the threat of change, there are central cults which reinforce the institutions of chiefship and the family. Persons unrelated to the chiefly family can be possessed by the spirit of a departed chief and then become a counsellor or wife to the reigning chief. Commoners, on the other hand, are frequently possessed by the spirits of their own ancestors. Among the Lugbara spirits are either ghosts or refractions of the Divine Spirit and change is accounted for as a concomitant of cosmological confusion.[11] Foreign forces, therefore, such as the Christian revivalist movement the Balokole, can be incorporated into the central scheme of Lugbara ideas. Among both the Lugbara and the Alur there is a considerable use of rhythmical techniques and medicines to induce a genuine state of trance in the medium.

The Shetani spirit possession guild is a movement that has developed among the Islamic Swahili peoples of the East African coast and which has spread into mainland Tanzania as a result of contact between the interior and the coastal region.[12] It is possible also that the spirit possession cults of the Kamba of central Kenya, who have extensive contacts with the coast, have been similarly influenced. The Shetani spirits are an explanation for a variety of illnesses and misfortunes, particularly barrenness and psychical and sexual abnormality. As such, they are an elaboration of the concept of malevolent spirits found in the Qur'an under their leader Iblis. African tradition divides the Shetani into a number of 'tribes' according to their region of origin, and there are numerous sub-divisions catering for the different types of sickness and affliction. Gray distinguishes broadly between the Jinns who operate at sea and harass fishermen and seamen, and the Shetani proper, who inhabit the land. Cory, however, divides the latter into the coastal Shetani and the mainland Shetani, reflecting different cultural preoccupations.

In minor matters divination is the responsibility of Islamic officials, such as the sheikh or Qur'an school teacher and the Qur'an itself is used in the process of divination. There is also an orthodox form of exorcism to which people can have recourse. When, however, the burden of misfortune becomes more intolerable, the sufferers have recourse to the traditional doctors and to rituals of possession which owe little to official Islam. These consist mainly in a seance, during which communication is established with the Shetani spirits, and in dances to entertain them. Often there is also the sacrifice of a goat. The Shetani guild employs a number of techniques for inducing the state of trance in the patient. Foremost among them is the use of inhalants, vapours and incense. When in the state of trance, the patient's gestures, as well as his words, are interpreted as messages from the Shetani.

The Shetani guild has spread far into central, western and southern Tanzania. Not only does it exist there in its own right, but it has strongly influenced local traditions of spirit possession in the matter of techniques. Probably the most famous of the Tanzanian guilds is that of Buswezi, already referred to.[13] In Unyamwezi this guild is particularly esteemed for its colourful costumes and virtuosity in dancing. Its songs also exercise considerable fascination. People join the Buswezi, on the recommendation of a diviner, to cure diseases or as a remedy for barrenness. They may also join it because it is a family tradition. Although the myths of the interlacustrine Chwezi are part of Buswezi lore, they are not directly linked to the royal histories of the Nyamwezi or to traditions of family piety, as in western Uganda. On the contrary, Chwezi heroes, such as Lyang'-ombe and Ngasa, are peripheral to the cosmology and historical traditions of the Nyamwezi, and offer a relatively new explanation for the prevalence of certain types of affliction which threaten social relationships or entail a loss of social status. The initiation rites of the Buswezi are lengthy and elaborate. Like many others they centre on the symbolism of the human cycle of life-death-rebirth. The novice is given Swezi parents and sponsors and a whole new Swezi family community. He undergoes a number of endurance tests, and there is a fair amount of horseplay and sex-play during the ceremonies. The climax is the trance of the novice, induced by medicines and vapours, without which it is impossible to become a member of the guild.

South of Unyamwezi, in Ukimbu, the most popular and widespread spirit possession guild is that of the Migawo (or Migabo).[14] Its cosmology derives from the peoples who live to the west, between Ukimbu and Lake Tanganyika. The Migawo spirits are thought to be the spirits of the lakes, and their leader is known as Katavi. Besides being responsible for barrenness, bodily deformity, abnormal birth and other misfortunes, they are especially blamed for epidemics of sleeping sickness and swarms of locusts, both of which have entered Ukimbu from the western lake area (Lakes Rukwa, Katavi and Tanganyika). The songs and ceremonies of the Migawo are either borrowed from authentic Kimbu guilds or from the Buswezi. The techniques for inducing trance strongly resemble those of the Buswezi and Shetani.

Basically, the Migawo serves the same purposes as the Buswezi. It assembles people whose misfortunes are the cause of a loss of status, and allows them to enjoy a new prestige in their societies. The Migawo spirits, however, are non-historical, and are far less personal than the Swezi spirits. Apart from Katavi, their leader, they are not known individually, and they are not the objects of religious respect or ritual. There are three stages, or grades, of initiation into the guild, and each lodge centres round a specialist doctor diviner who trains his own apprentices, besides initiating ordinary members who come to him as patients. These specialists have spread the idea of Migawo possession with an almost missionary fervour. Whereas, before the Second World War, the Migawo was unknown in Ukimbu south of the river Rungwa, it has now become well established in almost every village and is apparently still on the increase.

Christian reaction to spirit possession in East Africa has been interesting. Roman Catholics and Anglicans have tended to equate local spirit mediumship traditions very questionably with diabolical possession, but the Pentecostal churches have opened up possibilities for a *rapprochement*. Independent church movements have aimed consciously, or unconsciously at rebuilding the shattered, traditional societies, and spirit possession—in this case possession by the Holy Spirit—and speaking with tongues have been powerful ingredients in independency. What is even more remarkable is that Pentecostalism is now becoming respectable as a movement within the Roman Catholic and Anglican communions, although it has yet to make an impact on their congregations in East Africa.

12

Witchcraft and sorcery

The study of witchcraft and sorcery has held a considerable fascination for social anthropologists.[1] The world of witches and evil magic is an unfamiliar one for westerners today. However, those who are fascinated by the unfamiliar run the risk of making ethnocentric judgments and this is largely what has happened in this case. It has been assumed too readily that societies which believe in witchcraft and sorcery are socially unhealthy, and that there is a greater degree of fear, tension, disorder and immorality among them than among people who do not have these beliefs. It has been suggested that the strength and tenacity of witchcraft beliefs are indications of the degree of tension in society, and that when social tensions increase, witchcraft accusations become more abundant. It is probably true to say that, in the present atmosphere of social change in East Africa, tension is on the increase, particularly in towns and areas of re-settlement. Yet, although rituals connected with witchcraft and sorcery flourish in town while other rituals do not, it is difficult to relate them to an observable increase in tension. There is not necessarily more witchcraft accusation in towns than elsewhere.

Witchcraft and sorcery are a means of defining, locating or justifying conflicts in society, and, as such, they are not necessarily socially destructive. There is conflict in all human societies, but different societies come to terms with it in different ways. Equally, however much one may be opposed to these things, there is violence and oppression of the innocent in every human society. In one society leniency towards a murderer may be expressed in terms of penological theory or a philosophy of non-violence. In another society it may be expressed in terms of witchcraft belief—the assumption that most people who die at the hands of another have merited punishment as witches. Witchcraft and sorcery also offer an explanation for the experience of misfortune and help to render it intelligible and tangible. Misfortune thus takes on a concrete shape that makes it easier to deal with. Witchcraft and sorcery also offer an outlet for feelings of stress and aggression, and accusations against others can be a means of exculpation where misfortune is believed to be related to sin and guilt. Like spirit possession, witchcraft and sorcery beliefs may provide a means of coping with the threat of change, and Beidelman has suggested that witches may be innovators, possessing imagination and creativity—in fact, unsuccessful prophets.[2]

Divination is one of the pillars of belief in witchcraft and sorcery. Using spirit mediumship or magical techniques, it acts as a kind of switch-board, 'switching' the one who consults it on to one of the socially accepted levels of explanation. Divination brings fears, suspicions and conflicts out into the light of day and offers social approval for the course of action that is afterwards taken to resolve the problem. Malevolent, peripheral spirits, if not actually on the side of the witches, are uncertain allies in the struggle against witchcraft. One finds that it is the spirits of the central cults which uphold traditional morality and which operate against witchcraft in the divinatory forms of spirit mediumship.

The distinction which social anthropologists make between witchcraft and sorcery is a theoretical one, and may or may not be very useful in practice. Whereas the term 'sorcery' is used to refer to evil magic, symbolical techniques for harming or hindering other persons, witchcraft is thought to be an innate or inherent power in certain people to harm their fellow human beings at will. Probably in the majority of East African societies the witch is thought to be also a sorcerer, and it is generally reckoned that no one but a witch could be bad enough to practise sorcery. Among the Kaguru, Kimbu, Nyamwezi and Sukuma of Tanzania, the Gisu of Uganda and the Gusii of Kenya, there is no practical distinction between witch and sorcerer. For the Mbugwe (Tanzania), Lugbara and Amba (Uganda) the distinction has some social importance, whereas among the Nyoro (Uganda) and the Nandi (Kenya) sorcery is definitely a much more important concept.[3] Again, probably the majority of East African peoples view the witch as consciously rejoicing in his or her evil deeds, whereas in certain societies or on certain occasions the threat may be small enough to admit the idea of unconscious witchcraft and non-vindictive rituals for neutralizing it. Baby twins among the Kimbu, for example, are thought to be capable of be-witching their fellow twin.

Witchcraft can be studied sociologically at two main levels—the ideological level, and the level of its relation to the social structure. At the ideological level one can examine witchcraft beliefs as a system and the relation of this system to other systems of belief. At the other level, witchcraft beliefs can be related to the accepted image of the community, to patterns of conflict and aggression, accusation and counter-accusation. Ideologically, witchcraft beliefs constitute a kind of 'distorting mirror world' of actual human society, a collective nightmare. They are a collective representation of evil, uniting all that is most fearful and detestable. Horror is piled on horror in the effort to find symbolical expression for the idea of unremitting and implacable evil. Although, for reasons connected with the social function of the beliefs, emphasis may be put on one or another detail, there is, as in the case of religious beliefs, a remarkable homogeneity in ideas about witches throughout East Africa. Again and again the same fantastic and grisly stories reappear. Witches are ugly or deformed; they have dark skins and red, protruding eyes that can see in the dark. They walk upside down on their hands, go naked, make themselves invisible, and dance at night near people's graves. Their top teeth grow before their bottom teeth when they are babies. They ride on the backs of animal familiars or change themselves into animals, hyenas, jackals, screech-owls, chameleons. They 'send' wild animals to attack men or destroy their crops and possessions. They lust after human flesh and disinter corpses to feast on them or use them for medicine. They can make the dead rise from their graves, and they command companies of zombies who act as messengers of evil or work to make them prosperous. They conjure the spirits of the dead into medicine containers, usually animals' horns or tails—symbols of brute power. They attack people when they are sleeping at night and feed on their body-souls to make them sicken and die. They are responsible for crimes perpetrated by unknown persons. Above all, they operate secretly, insidiously and at night. They are a 'fifth column in society', a threat to the whole social fabric, to everything that is decent and worth living for.

Witchcraft and sorcery are often related to the system of religious beliefs. For example, the Gisu (Uganda) emphasize the essential duality of both religious and witchcraft powers.[4] Just as there are benevolent and malevolent spirits, so there are benevolent and malevolent supernatural powers wielded by human beings. For the Nyoro (Uganda) the conjuring of evil spirits into horns is closely bound up with the belief in 'black' *mbandwa,* while anti-witchcraft divination is bound up with possession by 'white' *mbandwa.*[5] The coming of Christianity has done little to lessen the power of witch-craft beliefs in East Africa. On the contrary, in some respects it has strengthened these beliefs. Emphasis on Satan in early missionary teaching has given witchcraft a new dimension and references to witches in preaching, instruction and even vernacular translations of the Bible have tended to confirm the beliefs.[6] Christian endeavour must be directed towards the reduction of conflict and towards positive explanations for misfortune, if any headway against witch-craft beliefs is to be expected. Direct attacks and denunciations quite clearly have a reverse effect.

Mary Douglas has shown convincingly that the witch-hunting mentality is characteristic of the type of society which is viewed by its members as a clearly bounded group.[7] Loyalty to the group is paramount and there are no half-measures in this loyalty. One is either in the group or outside it. Such an attitude is probably funda-mental to every form of witchcraft belief, but there are innumerable variations on this basic theme. The outsider-witch, representing a hostile group and operating at long range, is probably the type of witch that is least feared. The effectiveness of witchcraft grows in proportion to its insidiousness and it is the witch operating at close range within his own group who is feared the most. At its simplest, witchcraft accusation is a mechanism for breaking relationships. A good example is provided by the Kaguru of Tanzania where frequent accusations are made against women by their husbands, expressing the conflict of loyalties between the clan and the woman marrying into it.[8] Among the Gisu, men accuse agnates of their own generation, while women accuse their co-wives or their affines in all misfortunes connected with childbearing.[9] Accusations between neighbours are common in nearly every society, and they also occur between fellow villagers who are not necessarily neighbours and in situations of hostility between villages when village loyalty is at a premium. This is the case, for example, with the Amba of Uganda.[10]

The symbolism of witchcraft reflects the preoccupations of those involved in the process of accusation. In a society like that of the Kimbu (Tanzania) where hunting is a particularly favoured activity, the witch is represented as causing hunting accidents and sending wild animals to attack their victims. In societies where accusation is between co-wives and affines, the symbolism of the witch centres on sexuality and fertility. Among the Nyakyusa of southern Tanzania where accusation takes place between age-mates, whose interest in each others' herds centres on the feasts they share, witches are represented, especially as lusting for meat.[11] Although such ideas are common to the pattern of beliefs in almost every society, the emphasis in a particular community follows the image that people have of it.

Witchcraft accusation may also be the expression of hostility between factions. Beidelman reports this for the Kaguru of Tanzania, and Gray shows for the Mbugwe—also in Tanzania—that when witchcraft accusations take place between members of different lineages, this has the effect of strengthening lineage loyalty.[12] Witchcraft accusation is also a means employed by authorities to retain power and ensure conformity. Opposing factions and political rivals are thus easily silenced by it. The author witnessed an example of this kind of accusation during fieldwork in a Kimbu village in southern Tanzania in 1966. On this occasion a villager conceived the ambition to become one of the ten-house-cell leaders (*kumi-kumi*) and challenged the existing cell leaders on a number of issues. At length, he was accused of causing the death of the father of one of the cell leaders and was forced to quit the village with his family and supporters and go to live by himself in the forest.

On the other hand, witchcraft accusation can be used as a means of turning the tables on authority. Middleton reports that among the Lugbara (Uganda) it is an accepted way of questioning the authority of the elders.[13] Certainly, oral tradition in East Africa knows of instances in the past when such accusations were levelled against chiefs. In two separate chiefdoms of Ukimbu (Tanzania) during the nineteenth century, chiefs were so accused. One was Kisenselia, chief of Itenda, who was put to death, and the other was Mbeveta, of Wikangulu, who was exiled. In both cases their alleged witchcraft had resulted in the deaths of a number of their subjects. Nevertheless, it is sometimes recognized that a chief has the right to use sorcery against political rivals or enemies. Gray states that the Mbugwe of Tanzania have such an official sorcery, according to which chiefs perform magic to frustrate the rainmaking of rival or enemy chiefs. Official witchcraft is also known to the Mbugwe, whereby chiefs have the power to send animals or familiars to punish their enemies, and there are numerous myths which attribute such powers to chiefs in the past.[14]

To some extent, power is linked in the minds of many East African peoples with evil or malevolence, and chiefs, diviners and mediums, although they are normally highly respected members of society, can be plausibly suspected of witchcraft on occasion. In spite of this, much depends on the viewpoint of those making the judgment. The use of retaliatory magic is socially approved and there are even inherent powers to retaliate which are also accepted as good and which are not classed as witchcraft. The Nyakyusa offer a good example. The inherent power to harm others is known as 'the breath of men' when it is used beneficially to defend the village and punish wrongdoers, but its anti-social use is dubbed *ubulosi*, witchcraft. These inherent powers can be increased through drinking medicines. Moreover, as Monica Wilson records, Nyakyusa chiefs can be accused of witchcraft and can become victims of the 'breath of men'.[15]

The most common means of witch-finding is through divination by oracles and mediums, but the Nyakyusa of Tanzania have a tradition of carrying out autopsies to discover signs of witchcraft in a deceased suspect. Such autopsies are tests of confidence in the relatives of the dead man. To refuse to allow the operation is tantamount to admitting that there are grounds for suspicion.[16] Ordeals were very common in the past as a means of identifying witches. Among them were the various forms of boiling water ordeal in which the suspect had to retrieve an object from a pot of boiling water, and the poison ordeals. In the latter, poison was administered to suspects who either vomited the mixture and were judged innocent, or who sickened and died, judged and punished by the ordeal itself. Many peoples of southern Tanzania used the poison *mwavi* (*erythrophloeum guineense*) to give to suspect witches. Today some people, like the Kimbu, use the same poison in an oracle consisting of a ball of millet porridge with some white maize flour in the centre. The *mwavi* root is inserted into the ball and the whole is dipped in water. If the poison comes out into the maize flour, the suspect is deemed guilty. Since modern law enforcement has prevented the application of ordeals to human beings, people have felt more insecure, and one hears it said quite frequently that witchcraft is increasing because the sanctions against it are no longer effective. Retaliatory medicines against witches are often used but people do not seem to place much

107

faith in them. Ostracism of the suspect or moving away from the suspect's village or neighbourhood are quite common today and may be the way in which movements on account of other causes, such as low soil fertility, are worked out. Inter-personal conflicts and rivalries offer an explanation for crop failure, and consequently for the need to move to more fertile ground. This is certainly the case in southern Unyamwezi and Ukimbu (Tanzania). In the last analysis, however, only the death of a suspected witch gives complete security.

The experience of a growing insecurity where witchcraft is concerned was widely felt all over East and Central Africa, and it led to the development of wide-ranging witch-cleansing or witch-eradication movements.[17] Mention has already been made in Chapter 10 of the Maji Maji rebellion in Tanzania in the early years of this century. This was basically a religious movement that took its origin in a rite of witch-cleansing. During the 1930s the Mchape movement spread from Central Africa into south-western Tanzania, and in the 1950s the movement known as Chahuta spread throughout the same area. At about the same time Alice Lenshina, leader of the Lumpa Church in Zambia—another witch-cleansing movement—entered southern Tanzania and made contact with Bemba migrants from Zambia. Mbozi district, in south-western Tanzania, was the point of departure for a number of witch-eradicators in the early 1960s and these men travelled widely, visiting village after village.

Witchcraft cleansing employs many of the techniques of the ordeal, although its effects are usually less drastic. The cleansers or eradicators use different means of smelling out the witches, examining their reflections, making them drink a medicine, or 'frisking' the suspects with a cow's tail. The whole effect of witch eradication depends on its completeness. Everyone must attend the sessions, and any absentee is immediately suspect. Everyone must submit to the ordeal and to the cleansing ritual, if the ordeal reveals that he is guilty of witchcraft. Cleansers also profess to be able to discover hidden witchcraft objects or evil medicines, such as horns. Everyone is called upon to bring such objects to the public session and to destroy them, and the cleanser visits private houses to smell out the horns. Although such movements can give security for a time, it is ultimately impossible to preserve a homogeneous, witch-free community in an age of increased social mobility and cultural contact. This is the reason why such movements follow one another in waves, and why they ultimately fail to satisfy. It cannot be denied, however, that these movements are themselves agents of wider co-operation and contact. They are also the product of individual talent and enterprise which has its commercial aspect.

A variation on the travelling witch-cleanser is the specialist with an international clientèle. Such specialists are rare and must be gifted with extraordinary organizing ability, as well as with a wide knowledge of the geographical areas from which their clients come. One of the most outstanding specialists of this kind was the famous Chikanga who flourished in Malawi in the 1950s and 1960s.[18] Although he remained in his own country, clients poured into his village from southern Tanzania, from places as far away as Tabora or Iringa. Special bus services were arranged for his clients, and Chikanga even had a rudimentary registration process with officially stamped papers for clients who had consulted him. Given examples like that of Chikanga, it is difficult to maintain that witchcraft beliefs and accusations are socially counter-productive.

13

Case: The urban host tribe—
the Ganda of Kampala

Kampala City, the capital of Uganda, is situated near the centre of
the northern shore of Lake Victoria and is surrounded by the area
known as Buganda, the homeland of the Ganda people.[1] Buganda
occupies the north-western section of the lake shore, and consequently
Kampala lies on the eastern side of the region. The islands found
in the north-western segment of the lake also belong to Buganda,
and chief among them is the relatively large Sese group. Until the
abolition of the kingdoms in Uganda in 1966, Buganda was a highly
centralized kingdom, enjoying a size and influence greater than the
others. The traditional political centre of this kingdom was at
Kampala. The city is built on and among a series of rounded and
flat-topped hills and the surrounding country is green and well-
watered, every valley or depression containing a river or swamp. An
inlet of Lake Victoria comes up to within a few miles of the city
centre which has its own nearby harbour for lake steamers, Port
Bell. There is a continuous rainfall throughout the year. A pumping-
station at Gaba, five miles away, provides the city with filtered water,
and electricity is generated fifty miles away at the Owen Falls Hydro-
Electric Station. The Uganda Railway links Kampala with Nairobi,
Kenya's capital, and Mombasa on the Kenya coast. On the west it
stretches up to its terminus, Kasese, at the foot of the Ruwenzori
Mountains.

Already in the second half of the nineteenth century, when it was
first visited by European explorers, the palace of the Kabaka or
King of Buganda, situated on one of Kampala's numerous hills,
contained approximately 500 buildings and was the focus for a
population of about 20,000. The Ganda today number close on two
million, and of these some 159,000 live in Kampala City—7 per cent

of the total Ganda population.[2] The city is composed of a number of power centres, or centres of national dominance, situated on the hills. On the lower slopes of the hills and in the swamps and valleys between them are found the low-income residential areas and the commercial and industrial quarters. Thus Mengo Hill, where the Kabaka's palace was situated (now a military barracks), was the administrative centre of the Buganda kingdom. Kampala Hill (now designated as the site of the Headquarters of the Muslim Supreme Council) still possesses the remains of the first colonial fort. This was replaced by the Old Fort on the higher, nearby hill of Nakasero, on the summit and forward slopes of which are found today government offices and residences, Parliament Buildings, the High Court, Radio Uganda, the National Theatre and the main shopping and entertainment centre of Kampala. The banks and hotels are also concentrated in this area. Rubaga Hill is the site of the Roman Catholic Cathedral, Archbishop's residence and mission hospital, while Namirembe hill is the Anglican counterpart, with its Cathedral, church offices and nearby mission hospital. Nsambya Hill, formerly the centre of an adjoining Roman Catholic diocese, now possesses the Office of the Catholic Secretariat and Kampala's third mission hospital. The government hospital, the largest in the country, is situated on Mulago Hill. Makerere Hill is the site of East Africa's oldest university campus, while across the railway line lies Kibuli Hill and mosque, focus of Kampala's Muslim community. East of Nakasero Hill stretches the Kampala golf course which divides the high-class residential area of Kololo Hill from the rest of the city. Other high-income areas are found on hills east of the town—Muyenga and Mbuya—and south, on Busiga and Bunga hills.

The railway and industrial complexes are found in the low-lying areas, and there also are found the stadiums and sports grounds and the low-income areas of which Katwe, Kisenye, Kibuye, Kiswa and Wabigalo are typical. Until 1966 the city was divided into two more or less distinct administrations—Mengo, which contained the palace and parliament of Buganda, and Kampala-East which contained the offices and parliament of the national government. After the abolition of the kingdom, the two areas were amalgamated, and in 1968 the city boundaries were enlarged to take in a total of seventy-five square miles and to amalgamate four municipal authorities with the Kampala City Council. Greater Kampala thus includes today a large number of peri-urban settlements or villages, as well as the central urban agglomeration. Although the Ganda were always the majority group in Kampala, their majority was considerably larger in the old Mengo municipality than in Kampala as a whole, (62 per cent as opposed to 48 per cent in 1959, for example). The Ganda style of life, reflecting the highly productive Buganda region, with its massive share in Uganda's major cash crops of coffee and cotton, predominated in the old Mengo municipality. The creation of the new Greater Kampala has strengthened this predominance within the city. It was in Kampala-East, however, that the majority of non-Ganda lived, that the industrial area was situated, and that new housing estates grew up and new patterns of residence were created.[3]

In 1969 the total population of Kampala was 330,700, of whom 293,328 were Africans. This African population lives in various types of settlement. By far the greatest number occupy the low-income areas, in cheap—often dilapidated—housing. In addition to the areas already mentioned above, there are Mulago village, Makerere-Kivvulu, Kibuli, Kisugu, Ndeba, Nakulabye, Wandegeya, Kam-wokya, Makindye, Najjanankumbi, Bwaise, Kawempe, Natete and many more. Such areas are not simply residential; they also exhibit a wide range of economic activities and a full social life. There are markets, shops, workshops, car-mechanics, carpenters, tailors, hairdressers and an ever-increasing number of beer-halls and bars with a nomenclature reflecting current political and cultural ideals. There are also small plots for food crops and even pasturage for animals—activities carried over into town from rural Buganda. Probably more than 50 per cent of the population of these low-income areas is engaged in some small-scale economic activity, and there may be from 1,000 to 2,000 dwelling units in each. Most of the land is privately owned, and a very large proportion of the inhabitants are squatters. Such areas are an obvious health hazard and places of high risk for initiation to crime and deviant behaviour.

A fair proportion of Kampala's African population lives in compounds or 'lines', in accommodation provided by public services, for example, the military barracks at Lubiri (Mengo), Makindye and Mbuya, the police centres at Naguru, Nsambya and Kibuli, the prison staff quarters at Luzira, and the railway quarters at Nsambya. Apart from such compounds, no serious attempt was made to cater for low-income residents until the 1940s. Attention was focused, for political reasons, on the relatively high-income group of civil servants. In 1948 and 1949 the two housing estates of Nakawa and

Naguru were built with the object of providing good rented houses for a lower range of incomes. Since then the various housing schemes, such as the Ntinda and Nsambya home ownership schemes, and the blocks of flats at Bugolobi (now requisitioned by the army), have catered once more for people with higher incomes. The majority of Africans continued to live in the dilapidated low-income areas already described.

Parkin's distinction between host and migrant is still useful.[4] Briefly, the host people are those who are more committed to the city and who regard the city as culturally 'theirs'. These are, of course, the Ganda. Even if they themselves have not lived long in the city, or do not intend to remain there long, the ties with the immediate Buganda homeland are so strong and immediate as to make a definite impact on the outlook and way of life of the city. For many of the poorly paid wage-earners the income from allotments near the city or from their home farms may be greater than their wage, and there are numerous social and cultural ties with the surrounding country-side, for example, marriages, funerals, mourning and inheritance ceremonies. The presence of Kampala in Buganda affects the life of non-urban Ganda in its turn. Standards of living, improved by rural prosperity, follow patterns created in town, and it becomes increasingly difficult to make cultural distinctions between city and country-side. Ganda culture is developing more or less uniformly, and the influence of Kampala City is a factor in this development.

Very different, however, is the situation of the migrant who hails from a tribal homeland other than Buganda, and even, in many cases, from a country outside Uganda itself. His homeland is not only physically further away, but he and his people are culturally distant from the majority of town dwellers he finds in Kampala. He tends to be more attached to a culture and way of life that is unaffected—at least immediately—by the city. He is more impervious to city influences and he finds it necessary to affirm his own cultural and ethnic identity by creating, for example, ethnic associations in the city. The longer he stays in town the easier it becomes for him to find a *modus vivendi*, but he rarely marries a host girl, and is much more likely to form casual unions with host women until he can marry a wife from his own homeland. If they are numerous enough, migrants form their own tribal villages in the city. Thus the Luo from Kenya have created their own villages at Wabigalo and Namuwongo, known collectively as 'Kisumu Kidogo' (Little Kisumu, after Kisumu, the Luo town in Kenya). There is also a Kinyoro for members of the Nyoro tribe, situated near Katwe, and there are two places called Kiziba for the Ziba or Haya people from Tanzania, notorious as centres for prostitutes. From the tribal village the migrant may graduate to a multi-tribal location, in which he finds himself consorting with neighbours of his own ethnic group, and eventually, in a few cases, he may reach the high-income area in which ethnicity has little or no social importance.

In 1959 the Ganda represented 48 per cent of all the African population in Kampala-Mengo. The 1969 census has no tribal analysis, but in the enlarged Kampala those born in Buganda are 54 per cent of the African population. In 1959 the Kenyans, mostly Luo and Luyia, formed the second largest grouping, and this was still true ten years later. In fact, in spite of the enlarged city boundary, they had grown slightly from 10·9 per cent of the African population to 11·73 per cent. This proportion was probably much reduced in 1973. The Luo were always the largest Kenyan group and were employed in large numbers in the railways and in the hotel and catering trade. They achieved considerable prosperity and were the majority of householders in Naguru and Nakawa housing estates. They had a flourishing Luo Association and numerous independent churches of Luo origin. The disfranchisement of non-citizens in 1964 meant that the Luo were excluded from any voice in the municipal government, but further pressure was to be exerted on them under the Obote regime and under the government of the Second Republic. The expulsion of the Asians meant a reduction in opportunities for the kind of employment to which the Luo were accustomed, and early in 1973 resentment against the large Luo share in East African Community services such as the railways was voiced in the Ugandan press. Although intimidation was officially denied and the Luo Association expressed its loyalty to the Ugandan government, numbers of Luo did, in fact, leave Uganda. After the Kenyans, the next largest ethnic group in Kampala in 1959 were the Toro with 7·6 per cent. Ten years later those born in Toro were only 3·4 per cent, fewer than the migrants from Kigezi who were 4·6 per cent. Other tribes represented were 2 per cent or less, and this was true of the political refugees from Rwanda, Zaïre and the Sudan.

In 1969, Asians were 9·5 per cent of the total population of Kampala and most of the commerce and industry was in their hands. The Kampala Asians represented 39 per cent of the total number of

114

Asians in Uganda, some 80,000 all told. After the expulsion of the non-Ugandan Asians from Uganda at the end of 1972, and the threat to transport the few remaining citizen Asians to a poorly developed region of northern Uganda, it is probable that very few of the remaining 2,000 or so Asians are in Kampala. Europeans were only 1·2 per cent of Kampala's total population in 1969. Of these, the largest single group was British, with 2,797 and the next largest was American with 484. With the take-over of many British businesses and the departure of volunteers like the Peace Corps, these figures now represent approximately the total number of British and Americans in Uganda as a whole. The majority, however, are probably in Kampala. In 1969 there were fewer Arabs in Kampala than Americans, but even today, with aid from Libya and Saudi-Arabia, they are probably not very much more numerous.

In the decade 1960-70 employment rose in Uganda as a whole, and in Kampala City which had 40 per cent of the country's employment in 1970, it had a higher rate of growth than elsewhere.[5] This was in large measure due to the fact that the bulk of small-scale and informal employment was found in Kampala. Although the majority of wage-earners were employed in the public services, most of those in business were employed in concerns with less than ten employees, only some 2,500 people being employed in the industrial area. Despite the relatively high rate of job creation in Kampala, there was, nevertheless, a net increase in unemployment, and it was estimated that in 1970, 35 per cent of all males in Kampala were unemployed. This was basically because the city had grown faster than the number of jobs. In 1959 the area within the present city boundaries contained 157,825 people. Ten years later the population had risen to 330,700. In the low-income areas the biggest full-time occupation for the men was looking for a job. Only 25 per cent of the job-seekers went in for petty trading, partly because of keen competition, poor returns and the waste of time involved. Of the women, 60 per cent were unemployed and only 15 per cent were engaged in petty trading. The extent of prostitution is difficult to assess, but it exists at different social levels and is not an exclusive characteristic of the low-income areas. Independent women are fairly numerous and three out of ten houses are female-centred. On the whole, migrant job-seekers leave their wives and families at home, and if an unemployed man has a wife and family in town, it is either because they are farming a plot, engaged in trading, or because he has

115

recently lost his job. The under-fourteen age group of children is poorly represented in Kampala for this reason, but the adolescents and young adults are over-represented, either because they are seeking employment, or because they are looking for a place in one of Kampala's numerous government or private secondary schools. Lack of school fees and lack of employment are the two biggest problems for them.

In spite of the kinship network and the relative proximity, for most of Kampala's inhabitants, of kinsmen in the surrounding countryside, there is real hardship and privation for a large section of the city's population. Many people show signs of malnourishment and are, in fact, living in minimal circumstances. There are frequent moves of households within Kampala itself, and in the low-income areas there are, on average, two persons per living room. With so large a population of young adults there is a danger of mounting frustration in view of the lack of jobs and the difficulty of fulfilling educational aspirations.

A very interesting development has taken place in the wake of the Asians' departure from Uganda. The businesses formerly owned by Asians have now been allocated to Africans who were able to prove to the allocating committee that they possessed sufficient capital and expertise. Although many enterprises were allotted to military personnel from other parts of Uganda, particularly high-ranking officers, the bulk of the small businesses have probably gone to local people. Kampala has become, almost overnight, a more thoroughly African town than either of the other two East African capitals. The immediate short-term effects of the Asians' departure have been an increase in unemployment and a loss of tax-revenue to the government. The African businessmen, however, start with several advantages. Their assets have been cheaply acquired and their businesses—especially the shops—operate on a family basis with relatively small overhead costs. Although they have inherited the Asian businesses, they have not been given the Asian residences. On the other hand, the disadvantages are also heavy. For the time being, imports are restricted and skilled men are hard to come by. Although imports may begin to flow again soon, it will be difficult to find training facilities, and distribution and financing will remain serious problems. Prices are inflationary and it may be hard to find a clientèle in many cases, since the Asians bought and sold among each other. In these circumstances some African businessmen will make a success of their enterprises, especially those with sufficient capital and skill. Many, however, are bound to fail, and Kampala will probably witness the rise of a small, politically important, entrepreneurial class of Africans. It is difficult to foresee a solution in the near future to the major problems of the city, but with their experience and with the natural advantages they enjoy, it is difficult to see how the Ganda can fail to be at the centre of the city's overall development.

14

Case: The developing agricultural community—the Kamba of Kenya

The Kamba of Kenya offer an example of a fairly typical rural community, developing at an even pace and without any sudden social upheavals.[1] Theirs is a quiet revolution in which a number of different influences are making a gradual impact. The Kamba number just over one million, the second largest ethnic group in Kenya and one tenth of the country's total population. They are Bantu-speaking. Ukambani, their homeland, is situated in Kenya's Eastern Province and lies at an almost equal distance between Mount Kenya in the north and Mount Kilimanjaro, across the Tanzanian border, in the south. In size it is twice as big as Holland and about one fifth the size of Great Britain. To the north-west lies the country of the Kikuyu; in the north, the lands of the Embu, Tharaka and Meru. On the eastern side are the Galla; while the Nyika and Taveta occupy the territory to the south. In the south-west Ukambani marches with Masai-land. Machakos and Kitui are the centres of the two districts into which Ukambani is divided. Machakos District on the western side is fairly hilly. In the northern part of the district, in the vicinity of the Iveti Hills, the country is fertile and developed. Below Machakos town are the Mbooni and Kilungu Hills, which are forest areas recently planted with coniferous trees, but the rest of the district is bushland with stony, sandy soil, until recently infected with the tsetse fly. The Athi River flows in a wide curve around the northern end of the district and then sweeps south to become the boundary with the neighbouring district of Kitui.

From Machakos the ground descends to the river, and on the other side rises the Yatta Plateau beyond which lies Kitui. Again, in the north-east, in the vicinity of the Tana River, the land is fertile, but away to the east it is a scrub-covered desert, deteriorating through over-population and scarcity of water. In the north-east the country is practically desert and there is no real boundary. The Kamba of Kitui are sometimes called Athaisu.

Ukambani has two rainy seasons, a short one from October to December and a longer one from March to July. During the dry seasons temperatures can rise to 27°C and water is scarce. Lack of water is, in fact, the most general problem. Numerous bore-holes have been sunk all over Ukambani and irrigation schemes such as the Furrow, the artificial channel leading from the Athi River, have been dug.

The Kamba, according to tradition, took their origin in Giriama at the coast, and their ties with the coast have always remained strong. Before 1750 they had crossed the Athi River and moved to the Mbooni Hills which became their dispersal area. They are divided today into twenty-five dispersed patri-clans known as *mbai*. The clans have their own totems and avoidances, and each is divided into sections known as *mivia* or 'gates'. The *mivia* are divided into family-communities or 'houses', *nyumba*, and the houses are again divided into nuclear units, *misyi*. The family-communities are grouped, on the basis of proximity, into territorial clusters, each of which traditionally had its own men's club, recreation ground, place of worship, council of war leaders and elders. Traditionally there were no chiefs, but certain important traders, mediums or prophets exercised a greater influence than their fellows. Chiefs were a novelty introduced by the British colonial administration, as elsewhere in Kenya. Traditional Kamba society was stratified into various age-grades: children, circumcised youths, warriors, married men and elders. The final level of elder was again sub-divided into three grades which were achieved through a series of initiations and payments. The final grade of elder involved ritual or sacerdotal duties. The Kamba have always been shifting—cultivators, growing sorghum, maize, millet, beans, peas, potatoes, yams and cassava. They also grow some sugar-cane and bananas. Recently introduced cash crops are coffee, in the better watered north, and cotton in the drier southern regions. Some honey-collecting is done in the woodland areas. The Kamba also raise sheep and goats, and in the south, below the hills, there is a fair amount of cattle-raising. In Kitui, where water and pasturage are more of a problem, there is some seasonal movement of cattle. Most of the cattle are short-horned Zebu.

In 1892 the British opened a police station at Machakos, and in the following year a station was opened at Kitui. This was the beginning of the colonial administration of Ukambani, but it was not the beginning of contact between Kamba and westerners. Already in 1849 Johann Krapf, of the Anglican Church Missionary Society, had reached Ukambani.[2] In the early nineteenth century, Kamba traders were already visiting Mombasa and the coast, and one of them, Kivoi, agreed to allow Krapf to join his caravan on its return to Ukambani. Krapf crossed the Athi River and climbed up to the Yatta Plateau where, from a vantage point near Kitui, he became the first white man to behold the snows of Mount Kenya. After a brief return to Europe, Krapf was ready, in 1851, for his second expedition. His aim was to found in Ukambani the first in a chain of missions among successive peoples. Although he reached Kitui once again, his party was attacked by robbers and, with his friends and servants killed or dispersed, he was forced to abandon his dream. The CMS was not to return until after the First World War. Krapf's attempt was not the only abortive mission in Ukambani. The Scottish Industrial Mission tried to found a post at Kibwezi on the main caravan route through the Athi Plains in 1891, but it was removed to Kikuyu seven years later.[3] In 1892 the Leipzig Evangelical Lutheran Society opened a station at Ikutha, and three years later, another at Mulango. It was the Africa Inland Mission, however, founded by Peter Cameron Scott in the USA which was to do most of the evangelizing of Ukambani. This was an undenominational mission society of a fundamentalist bent, which counted among its members a fair number of Baptists and Adventists. Its first station was opened at Nzaui in 1895, and others soon followed at Kangundo in 1896, at Machakos in 1902 and at Mbooni in 1908. By 1934 the AIM had 3,675 members in Ukambani and twenty-two schools with a total of 1,185 pupils. In the 1930s the AIM formed the Africa Inland Church (AIC) for the African followers of the mission. Roman Catholic Holy Ghost Fathers began to deploy through Ukambani in the 1920s, placing their emphasis on education, and the Kiltegan Fathers later came to Kitui, where, in 1967 they had a church population of 12,455. Today, there are two Roman Catholic dioceses in Ukambani —Machakos and Kitui—with twenty-seven parishes between them. In addition to the denominations already mentioned, the Salvation Army and the Presbyterians also came to work among the Kamba and the CMS returned as well. John Mbiti estimates that today there are some 300,000 Christians of all denominations in Ukambani, with from 700 to 800 congregations.

In 1899 the railhead of the Uganda Railway reached the Athi Plains and the railway was officially opened in 1901.[4] The line runs parallel to the present Nairobi-Mombasa road along the south-western boundary of Ukambani. The coming of the railway had profound effects on the Kamba who had already established a reputation as long-distance traders and were now given the means of establishing contacts much further afield. The railway was also instrumental in bringing the city of Nairobi into being, firstly as the centre of the railway administration, and later as the developing commercial and industrial capital of Kenya. Obviously, the proximity to Ukambani of a city with half a million inhabitants cannot fail to have an impact on the Kamba, and the latter are an important ethnic group within the city. Strange to say, however, although Nairobi is little more than forty miles from Machakos, the Kamba still have more contact with Mombasa and the coast. Another important development for the Kamba was the recruitment of large numbers to the police force and even more to the army. The Kamba were the backbone of the battalions of the King's African Rifles raised in Kenya in colonial times, and are still an important element in the Kenya Army today. Army life not only suited the Kamba wanderlust, it also enabled many families to supplement a meagre agricultural income and—not least important—provided them with an education and even a trade. Although Swahili was, and is, the language of the Kenya armed forces, English is also taught. Among the numerous trades needed and taught by the army, auto-mechanics is probably the most important, and the Kamba possessed a special aptitude for mechanics.

Kamba were well-known as hunters in former times and they specialized in the use of the bow and poisoned arrow. They possessed poisons strong enough to drop an elephant. These techniques stood them in good stead in the hey-day of the ivory trade and were one of the factors which promoted their tradition of long-distance trade. In modern times the Kamba have developed a skill for wood-carving. The centre of the wood-carving industry is at Wamunyu, almost equidistant from Machakos and Kitui. With the expansion of the tourist industry in East Africa, there has been a corresponding expansion of the market for wood-carvings. The Kamba quickly responded to the opportunities provided and have produced a wide range of stereotyped curios of varying quality. These are peddled by itinerant Kamba traders all over East Africa at hotels, airports, the main streets of cities and wherever tourists gather. Itinerant Kamba traders can be met with even as far away as Zaïre or Rwanda and Burundi, besides the other East African countries. Latterly they have been hit by currency regulations which make it difficult to send their remittances back to Ukambani and transfer their earnings.[5] Kamba are also well known for their traditions of music and dancing, and their dancing troupes are in considerable demand for public displays and tourist entertainment.

In 1903 part of the south-west of Ukambani was allocated to European settlers who began large-scale farming in the area, along the lines of communication, road and railway. Cattle were raised for meat and dairy products, and there was some poultry farming. On the whole the European farms made little impact on the Kamba. Some new stock was introduced into the bigger African farms and some poultry raising on a commercial basis has been begun, but without any significant success. The European farms, however, attracted various industries in the Athi River area, chief among which was the Kenya Meat Corporation with its abattoir and meat packing plant. There is also a large prison and prison farm at Athi River.

In the Athi River area is found a type of crystalline limestone which is excellent for the manufacture of cement, and the factory of the East African Portland Cement Company began operating at Athi River in 1958. At Sultan Hamud, some fifty-four miles by road from Athi River, a mineral called vermiculite has recently been discovered. This is a kind of mica—magnesium aluminium silicate—useful in heat and sound insulating, and the vermiculite found at Sultan Hamud is reckoned some of the purest in the world. It has yet to be exploited, unlike the cement at Athi River which is Kenya's biggest export in terms of bulk and the country's ninth biggest money earner. Once again, the Kamba have been little affected by these industries and the majority of those employed by them are members of the Luo tribe from the Rift Valley Province.

A new development, however, which has had a much greater effect has been the Tana River Hydro-Electric Scheme, which is bringing about a gradual electrification and which is to supply electricity to Mombasa and the coast. Irrigation schemes and the drilling of bore-holes all over Ukambani have also made a difference.

More important, perhaps, has been the instilling into the Kamba of an ideology of self-reliance where farming is concerned. Traditionally, the only solution for the over-crowded rural areas was to seek an outlet through long-distance trade and military service. Today such solutions are no longer adequate in a rapidly growing population. Fifteen years ago, the population of Ukambani was little more than half a million. Today it is above the million mark. Self-help *Harambee* projects have been started all over Ukambani. One of the most common has been the installation of cattle-dips. Another has been the building of dams for the conservation of water and irrigation of farms. Other popular locational schemes have more to do with the quality of human life. These are the building of schools and dispensaries.

Basically the problem of providing for the growing population of Ukambani was one of land utilization and reclamation. The Kamba social system and system of inheritance did not pose any serious obstacle. Territorial clusters could form and re-form, and title to land depended both on ownership and occupation. An individual could alienate land, but was obliged to offer it to his family first. If the exhaustion and overstocking of the occupied land was to be overcome, it was necessary to eliminate the two traditional foes, drought and the tsetse fly. In 1932 in Machakos District a population of some 300,000 was cultivating a total of 140,000 acres, approximately one tenth of the existing land.[6] Much of the uncultivated land was rocky and sandy, or steep, uncultivable hillside, but between 200,000 and 300,000 acres could have been occupied were it not for the tsetse fly, the insect which transmits *trypanosomiasis* to cattle and to human beings. In 1937, a fly-belt one mile in width, was made to stop the tsetse invading the inhabited part of Machakos. In 1945 it was decided to clear the whole of the Makueni region of Machakos, thus adding another 250,000 acres to the area under cultivation, and settle the area with Kamba, under conditions of restricted grazing and modern cultivation. The first intention was to establish large co-operative farms, but the Kamba refused to be settled within their own homeland of Ukambani under any set of rules. The scheme was therefore exchanged for another of model 18-acre farms. Generally speaking, co-operatives have been weak in Ukambani and it was hoped that there would be less objection to the second type of scheme. The first reaction of the Kamba to the scheme was one of extreme suspicion, but eventually, by 1947, opposition to it was broken. Several government chiefs and successful Kamba farmers accepted model farms in Makueni and succeeded in persuading numbers of other families to move with them. It would be misleading to suggest that the Makueni scheme has been an unqualified success. The main problem was to get the Kamba to abandon a small, shifting 3-acre farm for a large, permanently and intensively culti-vated 18-acre one. This entailed an intricate and delicately balanced process of rotation, in some ways more difficult than the modern methods used by the Europeans in their extensive farms. However, the scheme is working today and produces a fair output of cotton, maize and beans. More interesting still, the Makueni settlement scheme has set off a movement of voluntary re-settlement. The clearing of Makueni was a massive operation, costing more than £67,000 in the 1940s. It also involved the shooting of about a thousand rhinoceros. As a result the tsetse has retreated, making the country safe to settle a long way further south. Kamba are now moving down of their own accord into lower Makueni and squatting in the country bordering the Tsavo National Game Park. Settlements are now growing near Makindu, Kibwezi and Mtito Ndei.

On the whole, the settlement areas are rather individualistic and there are few social centres or amenities in the area of the government scheme. In lower Makueni there was a scattered, older population with whom the settlers were obliged to mix. Generally speaking, the settlers still regard their place of origin as 'home' and have stronger social ties with this homeland than with the second home of the settlement.

Life has changed slowly for the better in Ukambani. There is a district hospital in Machakos and several smaller ones without a doctor. There are numerous government dispensaries. There are mission secondary schools and a few government secondary schools, in addition to a large number of Harambee schools. Primary school-ing is easy to come by. The perennial problems of Ukambani have been at least partially solved, and there is some prosperity. That this prosperity is in many ways a 'surface prosperity', since rural incomes are still supplemented by wages and trade-profits, in no way detracts from the very real developments that have taken place within Ukambani itself.

15

Case: A rural re-settlement area in southern Tanzania

It can be argued that the area chosen for study in this chapter is not typical of Tanzanian re-settlement areas in general. This may well be the case. On the other hand, few other places offer such a varied history of concentration and re-settlement, and few exhibit so clearly the problems connected with re-settlement. The area studied lies in the Chunya Area (District) of southern Tanzania, one of the four Areas that make up Mbeya Region (Province). The Area occupies 12,214 square miles and has an elevation of between 5,000 and 7,000 ft above sea-level. There are two seasons, a rainy season lasting from November to April, and a dry season from May to October. From twenty to fifty inches of rain falls each year, and apart from the months of June and July, the temperatures vary from 21° to 27°C. In June and July the temperature is around 15°C. Most of the area is covered with savanna woodland, consisting of trees of the *brachystegia* and *isoberlinia* species, and is infested with tsetse fly. In the south-west there is an open savanna plain surrounding the salty and evaporating waters of Lake Rukwa. Into this lake flows the Songwe River and its chief tributary the Lupa which rises in the north. Chunya, the Area administrative centre, lies in the south-east.

Over most of this area the people have traditionally engaged in small-scale, subsistence, shifting cultivation, carried out in palisaded farms and villages in the woodland clearings. Almost as important as agriculture are hunting and gathering, particularly honey collecting. In order to exploit the environment in the most effective way and to protect the cultivated areas from marauding animals, the villages are kept small. Although water is plentiful everywhere, soil fertility is low. Ecological factors therefore make the movement of villages necessary as well as possible, and the lifetime of the average village is about six years. In many cases, however, a village 'creeps' over the countryside, abandoning old farms and clearing new ones. There may thus be a continuity of identity over a long period of time between villages that have occupied different sites within short distances of each other. The principal crops are maize, millet, beans, peanuts, groundnuts, squashes, tubers and cassava. Poultry is kept, but the tsetse fly makes the raising of cattle impossible.[1]

Chunya Area has a population of about 50,000, of whom about one third live in the northern part known as Ukimbu. Most of these are members of the Kimbu tribe, but the non-Kimbu who have settled there are indistinguishable from the Kimbu. They are mostly from the neighbouring Nyamwezi and Bungu peoples whose way of life resembles that of the Kimbu. In the south-west, in the woodland region above the escarpment, and on the plain below it, live the Bungu, a people closely related in their origins to the Kimbu; while in the south-west are found the Guruka, in the neighbourhood of Chunya town. The former number some 20,000, while the latter, together with the population of the town, amount to some 12,000.[2]

The Kimbu of Chunya Area belong to two major groupings or associations of chiefdoms, the Nyisamba and the Nyitumba. The Nyisamba and dependent groups count a total of twenty-six chiefdoms in the Area, all deriving ultimately from the original chiefdom, Wikangulu, which was founded before the end of the seventeenth century. The Nyisamba live in the north and north-west. The Nyitumba, on the other hand, who are found in the eastern part of the Area, count four chiefdoms, among which Kipembawe is considered the founder. The ruling dynasties of the Nyitumba and Bungu peoples took their origin in the Itumba Hills of eastern Tanzania, and moved to the Chunya district during the eighteenth century.

During the early colonial period both the Germans and the British ruled indirectly through the traditional Kimbu chiefs, grouping their chiefdoms successively within different districts. In 1929 the British grouped the Chunya Kimbu within a specially created Kimbu district, known as Kitunda District, but this was abandoned in 1931. For the next three years the Chunya Kimbu were administered from Tabora in the north, while the Bungu and Guruka remained within Mbeya District (now Area) to the south. Then something happened which was destined to set in motion a series of social upheavals unparalleled in Kimbu history. Gold was discovered in the Lupa River and other tributaries of the Songwe, and a gold-rush took place which culminated in the creation of the Lupa Controlled Area in Mbeya District in 1932. The headquarters of this controlled mining area was situated in the growing town of Chunya and its officers were responsible for the affairs of the Bungu and Guruka. In 1934 the Chunya Kimbu were transferred from Tabora District to the Mbeya District and placed within the jurisdiction of the Lupa Controlled Area. Finally in 1942, the Lupa Controlled Area became Chunya District (Area). The Second World War administered the death-blow to the already declining gold-workings and Chunya became virtually a ghost-town. By contrast, the growing settlement at Mwambani in Ubungu began to assume greater administrative importance, especially with the opening of the District Hospital there in 1970. At the time of writing there is growing pressure to move the Area Headquarters to Mwambani.

Although the Kimbu were not directly involved in the gold-panning and mining operations on the Lupa, the immediate result of their being transferred to the Lupa jurisdiction was an ambitious plan to re-settle them in four major concentrations. The administration of tiny, scattered settlements was a problem, and it was hoped that the concentrations would make things easier. Ostensibly the creation of the concentrations was due to the threat of sleeping-sickness, in spite of the fact that an earlier government report had found no incidence of the disease of epidemic proportions in Ukimbu.[3] However, if the Kimbu themselves did not have to be protected against infection, there was a serious fear that the infection could spread to the mining areas with their heavy European, Asian and African populations.[4] During 1934, therefore, the administrative officer and agricultural officer toured Ukimbu and explained to the people the benefits of living together in large communities, and of abandoning forest pursuits in favour of agriculture.

One of the concentrations was to be at Kipembawe, on the recently constructed road which connects Mbeya with the central railway line. From the very beginning, the concentrations were a failure, and Kipembawe was no exception. Two Nyitumba chiefs (of Ilundu and Ilume) remained deep in the forest, east of Kipembawe, defying the order to concentrate. The senior Nyisamba chief of Wikangulu, however, moved with his people to Kipembawe, and a very explosive situation developed. The concentrations had been designed on geographical lines, and no reference was made to traditional loyalties. To subordinate the Nyisamba chief to the authority of a Nyitumba, regarded traditionally by the Nyisamba as a newcomer, if not a usurper, was ignominious in the extreme, and the Nyisamba chief deserted the concentration as early as 1938, with many of his followers. The remainder departed in 1949 when a large exodus took place from Kipembawe as a result of soil conservation measures enforced by the agricultural officer. Yet another exodus occurred when a police post set up in 1951 and a police campaign was waged against the illicit sale of beer. A handful of settlers struggled on at Kipembawe, but the soil was by now worked out, and the dozen or so householders who remained in the early 1960s were shopkeepers, or people employed by the health, game and public works departments. The Roman Catholic Mission which had opened in 1938, after several temporary closures, was finally abandoned in 1960. Many of the Kipembawe settlers, particularly the Nyitumba, moved south and set up a reasonably large village of traditional type on the main road, eleven miles from Kipembawe.

The independent government of Tanzania focused its efforts on bringing the Kimbu to the vicinity of the main roads, without expecting them to form large concentrations. However, it did not abandon the idea of re-settlement altogether, and in the early 1960s new plans were laid. It was discovered by soil experts that the light, sandy soil of southern Ukimbu was ideal for growing Turkish tobacco. Accordingly, it was decided to create two new, tobacco-growing settlements, one of them at Matwiga, four miles from the road-site of Mazimbo village. No direct attempt was to be made to re-settle the Kimbu themselves, but the settlements would be open to all comers and it was hoped that the Kimbu would follow the lead given by more enterprising people from the populous tribes of the southern highlands.[5]

The Matwiga Settlement was founded under the auspices of the Tanganyika Development Corporation and OXFAM, and the first step consisted in the survey of more than 5,000 acres by field officers of the Land Planning Division. The next step was to provide temporary accommodation for the first ten families. Settlers were then invited who had the following qualifications: Tanzanian citizenship, age of thirty or below, married status and physical fitness. The scheme began in 1963, and by February 1964, fifty settlers and their families had come to Matwiga. Each settler was given an acre of land on which he could construct no more than three dwelling houses. The rest of the land was to be hoed and planted with food-crops to feed his family. A reservoir was built and water was piped to taps at convenient distances from the houses. During the first year, food, housing, medical care and transport were provided free and settlers were exempted from paying local rates for three years. A fish-pond was also built and stocked with Tilapia fish. The whole village was placed under the surveillance of a manager who was a European for the first year, replaced in the second by an African.

During 1964, the major work consisted of clearing the forest for cultivation. Besides the residential area, four large tobacco fields had to be cleared for rotating the crop year by year. In 1965 every settler was asked to plant half an acre of Turkish tobacco in the first field, and a total of nineteen acres were cultivated. During the year the number of settlers grew from 50 to 150, (700 people in all) and the tobacco acreage was increased to 72½. The total income from the original nineteen acres was EASh. 24,350/30 and individual earnings ranged from EASh. 1,005/60 to EASh. 200 (£1 sterling is approximately EASh. 17). In 1965 the tobacco was dried on communal racks in the sun and in communal air-curing barns, but in 1966, the settlers began to construct their own fire-curing barns—high mud-brick structures next to their dwelling-houses. By 1966, there was a primary school at Matwiga, a dispensary, and out-station chapels for Roman Catholics and Moravians with resident catechist and evangelist. The political administration of Matwiga settlement, however, was not independent, and the new village came under the authority of the Village Executive Officer of Mazimbo and the Mazimbo branch of the ruling political party, the Tanganyika African National Union (TANU). During 1966 both Mazimbo and Matwiga adopted the ten-house-cell system of organization.

In 1966 there were already at Matwiga representatives of the Bungu, Nyamwezi, Guruka, Nyakyusa, Nyiha, Safwa and Sangu tribes. Only sixteen Kimbu settlers joined the scheme—little more than 10 per cent. Until 1971, settlers continued to join the new village, bringing the total to around 250. However, the Kimbu element did not increase appreciably. The settlers divided into two broad sections, the Kimbu and those who, like the Nyamwezi and Bungu, shared a style of life similar to the Kimbu on the one hand, and the southern tribes on the other.[6] Among the southerners, the largest group was that of the Nyakyusa. The two groups may be referred to as 'northerners' and 'southerners'. The northerners were more or less indigenous to the area and regarded the settlement as their home. The

129

majority had relatives living in neighbouring traditional villages, including, especially, Mazimbo. Although they were committed to the settlement, the northerners put less stress on its avowed purpose, —the growing and processing of tobacco. Many were still wedded to the forest pursuits which tobacco farming was intended to replace, and which, in the case of honey-collecting, conflicted with the tobacco processes. Just when the intricate work of picking, threading and curing the tobacco was supposed to take place, the northerners would be tempted to hang their hives in the forest and to go on long forest expeditions for this purpose, since it was also the moment when the bees were swarming to the nectar-producing trees. The northerners had little difficulty, however, in cultivating their food crops. They were used to the terrain, and knew how best to exploit the short-lived fertility of a woodland clearing.

The southerners were less committed to the settlement. For them, it tended to be a place of work rather than a home. However, they grasped the principles of tobacco farming more quickly and had no distractions to interfere with their main occupation. As a result, their incomes from tobacco growing were substantially larger. In any case, many of them, particularly the Nyakyusa, were originally more prosperous than the northerners and enjoyed a better standard of living. The northerners, on the other hand, were discouraged by the poor initial returns. In the first year of Matwiga's existence, the tobacco was sold to Rhodesia, but with the latter country's Unilateral Declaration of Independence, the second-year crop was bought by the Tanzania Tobacco Corporation at a much reduced price. At the same time, bee-products were still fetching quite a high price, making honey-collecting an attractive proposition. Recreational and social facilities were minimal in the settlement, and the social focus for most southerners lay in their homeland of origin.

One fact, however, forced the southerners to cultivate relationships with the villagers of Mazimbo. This was their inability to provide their own food. For many southerners it was easier to buy food locally, or to hire out their labour to Mazimbo people for a share in the food-crop. Local beer parties and beer clubs (*kilabu*) also attracted them to Mazimbo, but the fairly general contempt which they exhibited for the Kimbu, coupled with a prosperity that attracted the daughters of Mazimbo householders, provided the makings of an explosive situation. It had been the hope of the agricultural department that the presence of a tobacco-growing settlement in

Ukimbu would give a stimulus to tobacco growing in the traditional villages. But if the Kimbu settlers at Matwiga were half-hearted about tobacco, disillusionment in Mazimbo was almost universal after the first experiences. Only a very few faithful tobacco-growers continued in Mazimbo, despite various inducements offered by the agricultural officer.

Meanwhile, other difficulties beset the organization of Matwiga village. Because of the poor quality of the soil for growing food-crops, it was soon found that the settlers must move their dwelling-houses and farms, and that a 1-acre plot was completely insufficient. Already by the end of 1969, six years from the beginning of the scheme, the house-sites of the original settlers had to be abandoned, and new clearings, further and further away from the tobacco fields, were made. This meant, of course, the abandonment of amenities such as the water pipes and taps, and a greater dispersal of the dwellings from the central offices, store, school, chapels and dispensary. Little by little Matwiga began to take on the appearance of a traditional Kimbu village.

During 1971, new impetus was given by the government of Tanzania to the founding of *ujamaa* villages throughout the country. The basic principle of the *ujamaa* village is that the villagers operate a block-farm in which work and profits are pooled. Generally farmers or householders are found who are willing to co-operate, and to launch the *ujamaa* farm. Gradually more people are attracted to the scheme and a committee is elected which usually disposes of special government grants for launching the farm and which is empowered to take the overall decisions. This committee supervises the work and the sharing and spending of the profits. It was obvious that *ujamaa* propaganda should be made first of all in the government settlement schemes, yet it was in these very settlements that some of the toughest opposition was encountered. This was not surprising since one of the initial attractions of the schemes were the promises of high individual incomes, an objective which many settlers undoubtedly achieved. *Ujamaa* now demanded considerable confidence and sacrifice on their part. At Matwiga several factors militated against the introduction of *ujamaa*. One was the basic social division within the village, and another was the shape the village had come to adopt in order to solve the problem of living. At the first hints of *ujamaa*, a number of settlers abandoned the village and many more threatened to leave after the 1972 harvest. During this period no new settlers came to Matwiga, and the village shrank as a result of the departures. In spite of this, *ujamaa* was introduced under strong government pressure in 1971. In 1972, it was still very difficult to carry out fieldwork in the village and questions were received with suspicion as being connected with the introduction of the *ujamaa* policy. Early in 1972 'Operation Chunya' was announced in the national press. This plan included starting *ujamaa* in Mazimbo village, and bringing some of the scattered Kimbu groups from Wikangulu to the already existing *ujamaa* village at Matwiga. At the time of writing, the plan has not yet materialized.

It is interesting to reflect on all these government-inspired schemes of re-settlement in Chunya. Each in turn has had to come to terms with the social and ecological realities of Kimbu life. If re-settlement is to succeed, it cannot be a question of grafting a new branch onto an old stock. Rather it has to be an outgrowth of the old stock itself.

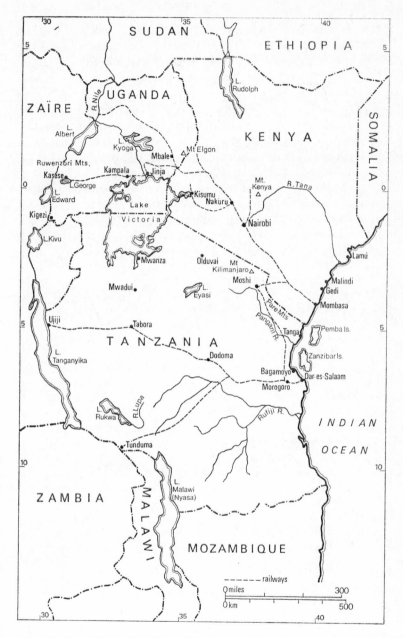

Map 1 East Africa, Physical and Political

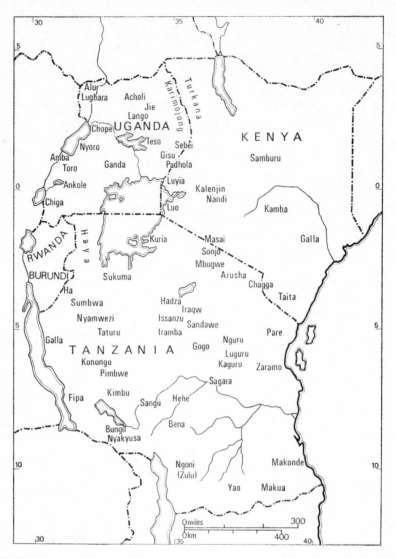

Map 2 **East Africa, Ethnic**

134

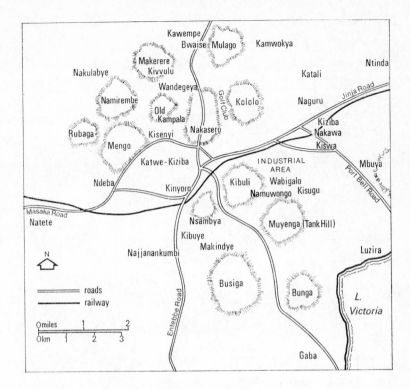

Map 3 **Kampala City, Uganda**

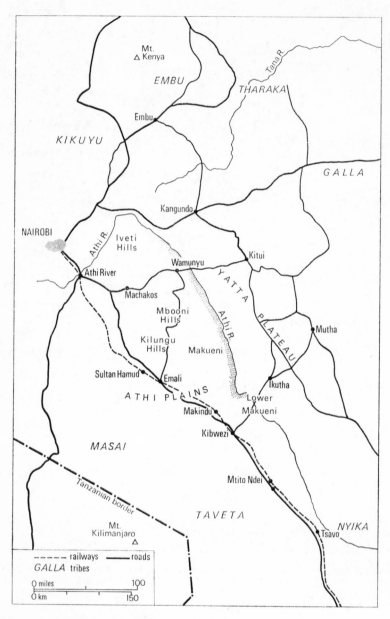

Map 4 Ukambani, Kenya

Map 5 Chunya **Area, Tanzania**

Notes

1 The anatomy of change in East Africa

1 A. Southall, 'The illusion of tribe', in P. C. W. Gutkind (ed.), *The Passing of Tribal Man in Africa*, 1970, Leiden, p. 28.
2 J. S. La Fontaine, 'Tribalism among the Gisu', in P. H. Gulliver (ed.), *Tradition and Transition in East Africa*, London, 1969, p. 188.
3 R. Cohen and J. Middleton, *From Tribe to Nation in Africa*, Scranton, Pennsylvania, 1970, p. 9.
4 Southall, op. cit., p. 44.
5 P. H. Gulliver, 'The conservative commitment in Northern Tanzania, the Arusha and Masai' in Gulliver, op. cit.

2 Ecology and demography

1 An excellent presentation of the physical environment is provided by *The Oxford Atlas for East Africa*, Nairobi and London, 1966.
2 For mining, industrial and other up-to-date economic information about East Africa, the reader will do well to refer to the volumes of *Africa: The Reference Volume on the African Continent*, *Jeune Afrique*, Paris and *Africa Journal*, London. The volumes for 1970 and 1971 were consulted for the preparation of this chapter.
3 For population figures, see Population Census Reports, published by the East African Statistical Department, Nairobi.

3 Peopling theories and short history

1 C. G. Seligman, *The Races of Africa*, Oxford, 1930.
2 Sheikh Anta Diop, *Nations Nègres et culture*, Paris, 1954.
3 H. Baumann and D. Westermann, *Les Peuples et les civilisations de*
4 *l'Afrique*, Paris, 1948.
 J. C. Trevor, *Race Crossing in Man*, Cambridge, 1953.
5 A good short description of the peopling of East Africa is that by J. E. G. Sutton in I. N. Kimambo and A. J. Temu (eds), *A History of Tanzania*, Nairobi, 1969, pp. 1–13.

138

6 M. Guthrie, 'Some developments in the pre-history of the Bantu languages', *Journal of African History*, 1962, III, pp. 273–82.

7 J. H. Greenberg, *The Languages of Africa*, Bloomington, Indiana, 1966; 'Linguistic evidence regarding Bantu origins', *Journal of African History*, 1972, XIII, pp. 189–216.

8 A good study of the comparative evidence from linguistics, archaeology and anthropobiology is provided by J. Hiernaux, 'Bantu expansion, the evidence from physical anthropology confronted with linguistic and archaeological evidence', *Journal of African History*, 1968, IX, pp. 505–16.

9 An important study of the Chwezi-Swezi traditions is L. de Heusch, *Le Rwanda et la civilisation interlacustre*, Brussels, 1966.

10 G. S. P. Freeman-Grenville, *East African Coast*, Oxford, 1962, pp. 146–51.

11 See R. Coupland, *East Africa and Its Invaders*, Oxford, 1938, and G. S. P. Freeman-Grenville, *The Medieval History of the Coast of Tanganyika*, Oxford, 1962.

12 For fuller accounts of East African history see The Oxford History; R. Oliver and G. Mathew (eds), *History of East Africa*, vol. I, Oxford, 1963, and V. Harlow and E. M. Chilver (eds), vol. II, Oxford, 1965.

13 A popular account of the East African Campaign is B. Gardner, *German East*, London, 1963.

14 For a concise account of recent East African history up to independence, see A. J. Hughes, *East Africa: The Search for Unity*, Harmondsworth, 1963.

4 Conservative pastoral societies

1 I am grateful to Professor Peter Rigby of Makerere University, Uganda, whom I consulted about this chapter.

2 See P. Rigby, 'The symbolic role of cattle in Gogo ritual', in T. O. Beidelman, (ed.), *The Translation of Culture*, London, 1971, pp. 257–91.

3 Michel Kayoya, *Sur les Traces de mon père*, Bujumbura, 1968, p. 31.

4 See P. Spencer, 'The function of ritual in the socialization of the Samburu Moran', in P. Mayer, (ed.), *Socialization, the Approach from Social Anthropology*, London (ASA 8), 1970, pp. 127–57.

5 Information on the Jie and Karimojong is taken from P. H. Gulliver, *The Family Herds*, London, 1955, and N. Dyson-Hudson, *Karimojong Politics*, Oxford, 1966.

6 Information on the Turkana is taken from Gulliver, op. cit.

7 See G. W. B. Huntingford, *The Nandi of Kenya*, London, 1953.

8 For the Arusha see P. H. Gulliver, *Social Control in an African Society*, London, 1963 and 'The conservative commitment in Northern Tanzania, the Arusha and Masai', in P. H. Gulliver (ed.), *Tradition and Transition in East Africa*, London, 1969, pp. 223–42.

9 For the Gogo see P. Rigby, *Cattle and Kinship among the Gogo*, Ithaca and London, 1969.

10 For the economic aspect of cattle raising, see René Dumont, 'Sentimental versus modern livestock raising', in *False Start in Africa*, London, 1966, pp. 172–87.

5 Chieftain societies

1 J. G. Frazer, *The Golden Bough*, London, 1922 (one volume abridgment).
2 R. Oliver and J. D. Fage, *A Short History of Africa*, Harmondsworth, 1962, p. 44.
3 E. L. Meyerowicz, *At the Court of an African King*, New York, 1962.
4 R. Oliver and G. Mathew (eds), *History of East Africa*, vol. I, Oxford, 1963, pp. 169–211.
5 Ibid.
6 E. E. Y. Evans-Pritchard, 'The divine kingship in the Nilotic Sudan', in *Essays in Social Anthropology*, Oxford, 1962, pp. 84–5.
7 M. Fortes and E. E. Y. Evans-Pritchard (eds), *African Political Systems*, Oxford, 1940.
8 A. Southall, *Alur Society*, Cambridge, 1953.
9 M. G. Smith, 'On segmentary lineage systems', *Journal of the Royal Anthropological Institute*, 1956, 86, ii, pp. 39–80.
10 See A. Shorter, *Chiefship in Western Tanzania*, Oxford, 1972.
11 Ibid., pp. 227–316.
12 A. Redmayne, 'The Hehe', in A. Roberts (ed.), *Tanzania Before 1900*, Nairobi, 1968, pp. 37–58.
13 See Shorter op. cit., pp. 264–316.
14 See J. Roscoe, *The Baganda*, London, (2nd ed.), 1965, and J. H. M. Beattie, *The Nyoro State*, Oxford, 1971.
15 L. de Heusch, *Le Rwanda et la civilisation interlacustre*, Brussels, 1966.

6 Urbanization

1 A number of works exist that deal with urbanization in Africa in general, and in East Africa in particular. This chapter has drawn on many of them. Examples are: W. Elkan, *Migrants and Proletarians*, London, 1960; P. H. Gulliver (ed.), *Tradition and Transition in East Africa*, London, 1969; J. A. K. Leslie, *A Survey of Dar-es-Salaam*, London, 1963; H. Miner (ed.), *The City in Modern Africa*, London, 1967; W. T. W. Morgan, *Nairobi City and Region*, London, 1967; N. Oram, *Towns in Africa*, London, 1965; D. Parkin, *Neighbours and Nationals in an African City Ward*, London, 1969; A. W. Southall and P. J. Gutkind, *Townsmen in the Making*, Kampala, 1957.
2 See A. W. Southall, 'Kampala-Mengo', in Miner, op. cit., pp. 297–332.
3 L. Swantz, 'Dar-es-Salaam Urban Worker's Handbook' (mimeographed notes), 1967.
4 See Parkin, op. cit.
5 L. Swantz, 'Communication between the urban and rural Zaramo in Dar-es-Salaam Area' (mimeographed), n.d.

6 Dr J. Orley develops the idea of traditional diseases in *Culture and Mental Illness*, Nairobi, 1970.

7 L. Swantz, 'Problems of development in urban areas' (mimeographed), 1968, p. 6.

8 P. Rigby and F. Lule, 'Divination and healing in peri-urban Kampala', (mimeographed), 1971.

9 Leslie, op. cit., p. 3.

10 This final section owes much to A. W. Southall, *Social Change in Modern Africa*, 1961, Oxford, pp. 22–53.

7 The rural revolution

1 This chapter is based mainly on fieldwork experience in rural Tanzania, on information gained during a stay of six years in Uganda and on visits during that period to Kenya. In particular, I am indebted to an unpublished report on a southern Tanzanian villagization scheme by my assistant Mr J. A. Mwaulambo, and to a mimeographed report on a similar scheme in which *ujamaa* is being introduced, made by Mr Njelu M. Kasaka of the University of Dar-es-Salaam.

2 These figures were quoted by Dr Addeke Boerma, Director-General of FAO. See *Comment*, CIIR, London, no. 7, pp. 2–3.

3 *Wajamaa*, the noun formed from *ujamaa*, means members of an *ujamaa* village.

8 Marriage and family life

1 See T. O. Beidelman, *The Matrilineal Peoples of Eastern Tanzania*, London, 1967, p. xiv.

2 M. Douglas, 'Is matriliny doomed in Africa?' in M. Douglas and P. M. Kaberry (eds), *Man in Africa*, London, 1969, pp. 121–36.

3 G. Enderley, 'Factors contributing to marital harmony and disharmony' (mimeographed paper read to All Africa Conference of Churches Consultation on Challenges of Family Education in Africa, Yaoundé, Cameroun), 1972.

4 A. Shorter, 'Marriage and attitudes to marriage among Christians in rural Uganda' (mimeographed circular of the Churches Research on Marriage in Africa), 1973.

5 See A. Hastings, *Christian Marriage in Africa*, London, 1973.

9 Socialization and education

1 Ideas for this chapter have been taken from papers on education in East Africa presented at past conferences of the East African Institute of Social Research, from relevant articles in Philip Mayer (ed.), *Socialization, the Approach from Social Anthropology* (ASA 8), London, 1970, and essays in L. Fox (ed.), *East African Childhood*, Nairobi, 1967.

2 For northern Ghana, see E. Goody, 'Kinship fostering in Gonja', in Mayer, op. cit., pp. 51–74.

3 Some material in this paragraph is taken from a lecture on traditional education given at Gaba Pastoral Institute in 1970 by Mr J. Gwayam-badde.
4 See D. Court, 'The social function of formal schooling in Tanzania' (mimeographed paper presented to the Universities Social Sciences Council Conference, Makerere), 1971.

10 Religious trends

1 See Okot p'Bitek, *The Religion of the Central Luo*, Nairobi, 1971.
2 See R. Harjula, *God and the Sun in Meru Thought*, Helsinki, 1969.
3 For example John Mbiti has several stories about salvation from the *iimu* in *Akamba Stories*, Oxford, 1966. The Master or Masters of the Animals, are called variously, *ilimu, ilimungala, idimungala simungala, mdimi* or *mudimi*.
4 M. Wilson, *The Communal Rituals of the Nyakyusa*, Oxford, 1959.
5 P. Rigby, 'The symbolic role of cattle in Gogo ritual', in T. O. Beidel-man (ed.), *The Translation of Culture*, London, 1971.
6 See J. S. Trimingham, *Islam in East Africa*, London, 1962.
7 I am indebted to ideas from F. Welbourn and L. Pirouet on the subject of the sociological aspect of conversion in East Africa.
8 T. O. Ranger, 'Missionary adaptation of African religious institutions: the Masasi case', in T. O. Ranger, and I. N. Kimambo (eds), *The Historical Study of African Religion*, London, 1972.
9 H. W. Turner, 'A typology for African religious movements', *Journal of Religion in Africa*, 1967, vol. I, no. 1, pp. 1-34.
10 F. B. Welbourn and A. Ogot, *A Place to Feel at Home*, Oxford, 1966.

11 Spirit possession and communities of affliction

1 For this chapter I have drawn largely upon J. Beattie and J. Middleton (eds), *Spirit Mediumship and Society in Africa*, London, 1969.
2 V. Turner, *The Ritual Process*, London, 1969.
3 V. Turner, *The Drums of Affliction*, Oxford, 1968.
4 M. Douglas, *Natural Symbols*, London, 1970, p. 65.
5 I. M. Lewis, 'Spirit possession and deprivation cults', *Man*, 1, 1966, pp. 307-29.
6 A. Southall, 'Spirit possession and mediumship among the Alur', in Beattie and Middleton, op. cit., p. 267.
7 L. de Heusch, *Le Rwanda et la civilisation interlacustre*, Brussels, 1966, works out the inter-relationship of the Chwezi traditions.
8 J. Beattie, 'Spirit mediumship in Bunyoro' and F. B. Welbourn, 'Spirit initiation in Ankole and a Christian spirit movement in western Kenya', in Beattie and Middleton, op. cit., pp. 159, 290.
9 I investigated this Christian version of the Chwezi cult on a short trip to the Ibanda area of Ankole in 1971.
10 Southall, op. cit.
11 J. Middleton, 'Spirit possession among the Lugbara', in Beattie and Middleton, op. cit., pp. 220-31.

12 R. F. Gray, 'The Shetani cult among the Segeju of Tanzania' in Beattie and Middleton, op. cit., pp. 171–87, and H. Cory (H. Koritschoner), 'Ngoma ya Sheitani', *Journal of the Royal Anthropological Institute*, 1936, LXVI, pp. 209–17.

13 R. E. S. Tanner, 'The theory and practice of Sukuma spirit mediumship' in Beattie and Middleton, op. cit., pp. 273–89.

14 A. Shorter, 'The Migawo: peripheral spirit possession and Christian prejudice', *Anthropos*, 1970, 65, pp. 110–26.

12 Witchcraft and sorcery

1 This chapter owes much to the introduction by Mary Douglas to the volume she edited, *Witchcraft Confessions and Accusations* (ASA 9), London, 1970.

2 See T. O. Beidelman in ibid., pp. 351–6.

3 These examples are taken from articles in J. Middleton and E. H. Winter (eds), *Witchcraft and Sorcery in East Africa*, London, 1963.

4 J. La Fontaine, 'Witchcraft in Bugisu', in ibid., pp. 187–220.

5 J. Beattie, 'Sorcery in Bunyoro', in ibid., pp. 27–56.

6 T. O. Beidelman, 'Witchcraft in Ukaguru', in ibid., pp. 57–98.

7 M. Douglas, *Natural Symbols*, London, 1970.

8 Beidelman, loc. cit.

9 La Fontaine, loc. cit.

10 E. H. Winer, 'The enemy within: Amba witchcraft and sociological theory', in Middleton and Winter op. cit., pp. 277–99.

11 Middleton and Winter, in the introduction to ibid., pp. 6–7.

12 See articles in ibid. See also A. Harwood, *Witchcraft, Sorcery and Social Categories among the Safwa*, Oxford, 1970.

13 J. Middleton, 'Witchcraft and sorcery in Lugbara', in Middleton and Winter, op. cit., pp. 257–76.

14 R. F. Gray, 'Some structural aspects of Mbugwe witchcraft', in ibid., pp. 143–74; also, A. Shorter, *Chiefship in Western Tanzania*, Oxford, 1972, pp. 154–6.

15 M. Wilson, *Communal Rituals of the Nyakyusa*, Oxford, 1959, *passim*.

16 Ibid.

17 R. G. Willis, 'Instant millennium: the sociology of African witch-cleansing cults', in Douglas (ed.) op. cit. (ASA 9), pp. 129–40.

18 A. Redmayne, 'Chikanga, an African diviner with an international reputation', in ibid., pp. 103–28.

13 Case: The urban host tribe—the Ganda of Kampala

1 This chapter draws on A. W. Southall and P. J. Gutkind, *Townsmen in the Making*, Kampala, 1957; A. W. Southall, 'Kinship, friendship and the network of relations in Kisenyi, Kampala' in A. W. Southall (ed.), *Social Change in Modern Africa*, London, 1961, pp. 217–29; and A. W. Southall, 'Kampala-Mengo' in H. Miner (ed.), *The City in Modern Africa*, London, 1965.

2 This and subsequent statistics are taken from *The Report on the 1969 Population Census*, vol. I, 1971; vol. II, 1973, Government Printer, Entebbe.

3 This paragraph and some of the later material on the low-income areas is taken from the UNICEF Report on *Kampala's Children*, Kampala (mimeographed), 1972.

4 See D. Parkin, *Neighbours and Nationals in an African City Ward*, London, 1969, and D. Parkin, 'Tribe as fact and fiction in an East African city', in P. H. Gulliver (ed.), *Tradition and Transition in East Africa*, London, 1969, pp. 273–96.

5 This section and some of the final projections are taken from C. Elliott, *Employment and Income Distribution in Uganda*, Development Studies Discussion Paper, University of East Anglia (mimeographed), 1973.

14 Case: The developing agricultural community—the Kamba of Kenya

1 For this chapter I have relied on J. Middleton and G. Kershaw, *The Kikuyu and Kamba of Kenya*, Ethnographic Survey of Africa, London, 1965; also on communications from informants with a knowledge of Ukambani, chief among them the Rev. Peter Suttle. I visited Ukambani briefly in 1972.

2 The story of Krapf's visits is re-told by R. Coupland in *East Africa and Its Invaders*, Oxford, 1956, pp. 408–20.

3 A good summary of missionary expansion in Ukambani is given by John Mbiti, himself a Kamba, in his *New Testament Eschatology in an African Background*, Oxford, 1971, pp. 10–16. His book discusses at length a subject not broached in this chapter, namely, the impact of Kamba traditional beliefs and Christianity upon each other.

4 The coming of the railway to Ukambani is described in J. H. Patterson's exciting book *The Man-Eaters of Tsavo*, London, 1907.

5 Interview with some itinerant Kamba wood carvers in Kampala on 5 June 1973.

6 See Middleton and Kershaw, op. cit., and a contemporary account of the start of the Makueni settlement scheme in N. Farson, *Last Chance in Africa*, London, 1949, pp. 195–203.

15 Case: A rural re-settlement area in southern Tanzania

1 Much of this chapter is based on A. Shorter, *Chiefship in Western Tanzania*, Oxford, 1972. This book was the outcome of fieldwork carried out in Ukimbu from 1964 to 1967, from 1968–9, and again for a short period from the end of 1969–70. The fieldwork was sponsored by the Nuffield Foundation. Finally, in 1972, my assistant, Mr Njelu Kasaka, carried out a month's research in two Chunya re-settlement areas.

2 I have obtained some information from an unpublished paper by Mr Joseph A. Mwaulambo, 'Community development in Chunya district', 1965.

3 National Archives of Tanzania (NAT), Early Secretariat, 7986/1, 61, Buchanan to Sleeping Sickness Officer, Tabora, 16 July 1926.
4 *Provincial Commissioners' Reports*, Iringa, 1935, p. 23.
5 My assistant Mr Joseph A. Mwaulambo carried out a study of Matwiga in 1965–6. Cf. his unpublished paper, 'The impact of villagization on traditional society in Ukimbu', 1966.
6 See Njelu Kasaka, 'Patterns of marriage in rural re-settlement areas' (unpublished pilot survey of Matwiga and Lupa Tinga-Tinga), 1972.

Further reading

GULLIVER, P. H. ed. (1967) *Tradition and Transition in East Africa*, London. This is a symposium by a number of experts, each dealing with a particular aspect of East African social life from the point of view of change and of the tension between traditional and modern life.

MIDDLETON, J. and WINTER, E. H. (1963) *Witchcraft and Sorcery in East Africa*, London. This is another symposium, more specialized than the first. The theoretical part of the book—the introduction—is open to criticism on a number of points, but the individual articles offer a picture of witchcraft beliefs in many East African societies.

The Oxford History of East Africa, offers essential background material for the study of East Africa. The first volume, edited by Roland Oliver and Gervase Mathew in 1963, deals with the pre-colonial era. Although the main lines still stand, it needs to be supplemented by a reading of the reports of more recent research.

ROBERTS, A. ed. (1968) *Tanzania Before 1900*, Nairobi. This is an example of a book giving more recent ethno-historical research findings. It is the fruit of a spate of research that took place in Tanzania at about the time when the Oxford History first appeared. It contains important new material which is just beginning to be absorbed into books for the more general reader.

SOUTHALL, A. W. (1953) *Alur Society*, Cambridge. This is one of the classics of East African political anthropology. It offers to the researcher the important model of the 'segmentary state', a concept that has been useful for the study of a large number of chieftain societies in East Africa, particularly in Uganda and Tanzania.

SOUTHALL, A. W. and GUTKIND, P. J. (1957) *Townsmen in the Making*, Kampala. This study of urban Kampala was published by the Makerere (formerly East African) Institute of Research and enumerates the main factors and trends in urbanization in East Africa. In spite of the increasing number of urban studies the book remains valuable.

WELBOURN, F. B. and OGOT, A. (1966) *A Place to Feel at Home*, Oxford. The authors study East African independent church movements in this volume and offer sociological explanations for their coming into existence.

146

Bibliography

BAUMANN, H. and WESTERMANN, D. (1948) *Les Peuples et les civilisations de l'Afrique*, Paris.

BEATTIE, J. and MIDDLETON, J. eds (1969) *Spirit Mediumship and Society in Africa*, London.

BEIDELMAN, T. O. (1967) *The Matrilineal Peoples of Eastern Tanzania*, London.

BEIDELMAN, T. O. ed. (1971) *The Translation of Culture*, London.

COHEN, R. and MIDDLETON, J. eds (1970) *From Tribe to Nation in Africa*, Scranton, Pennsylvania.

COUPLAND, R. (1938) *East Africa and Its Invaders*, Oxford (2nd edition 1956).

DOUGLAS, M. (1970) *Natural Symbols*, London.

DOUGLAS, M. ed. (1970) *Witchcraft Confessions and Accusations*, ASA 9, London.

DOUGLAS, M. and KABERRY, P. M. eds (1969) *Man in Africa*, London.

DUMONT, R. (1966) *False Start in Africa*, London.

ELKAN, W. (1960) *Migrants and Proletarians*, London.

ELLIOTT, C. (1973) *Employment and Income Distribution in Uganda*, University of East Anglia.

EVANS-PRITCHARD, E. E. Y. (1962) *Essays in Social Anthropology*, Oxford.

FORTES, M. and EVANS-PRITCHARD, E. E. Y. eds (1940) *African Political Systems*, Oxford.

FRAZER, J. G. (1922) *The Golden Bough*, London (1 volume abridgment).

FREEMAN-GRENVILLE, G. S. P. (1962) *The East African Coast*, Oxford.

FREEMAN-GRENVILLE, G. S. P. (1962) *The Medieval History of the Coast of Tanganyika*, Oxford.

GARDNER, B. (1963) *German East*, London.

GREENBERG, J. H. (1966) *The Languages of Africa*, Bloomington, Indiana.

GULLIVER, P. H. (1955) *The Family Herds*, London.

GULLIVER, P. H. (1963) *Social Control in an African Society*, London.

GULLIVER, P. H. ed. (1967) *Tradition and Transition in East Africa*, London.

HARJULA, R. (1969) *God and the Sun in Meru Thought*, Helsinki.

HASTINGS, A. (1973) *Christian Marriage in Africa*, London.

HEUSCH, L. de (1966) *Le Rwanda et la civilisation interlacustre*, Brussels.

HIERNAUX, J. (1968) 'Bantu expansion—the evidence from physical anthropology confronted with linguistic and archaeological evidence', *Journal of African History*, XIII, pp. 189–216.

HUGHES, A. J. (1963) *East Africa, The Search for Unity*, Harmondsworth.

HUNTINGFORD, G. W. B. (1953) *The Nandi of Kenya*, London.

JEUNE AFRIQUE (1970) *Africa: The Reference Volume on the African Continent*, Paris (also the volume for 1971).

KIMAMBO, I. N. and TEMU, A. J. eds (1969) *A History of Tanzania*, Nairobi.

LESLIE, J. A. K. (1963) *A Survey of Dar-es-Salaam*, London.

LEWIS, I. M. (1966) 'Spirit possession and deprivation cults', *Man*, 1, pp. 307–29.

MAYER, P. ed. (1970) *Socialization, the Approach from Social Anthropology*, ASA 8, London.

MBITI, J. (1966) *Akamba Stories*, Oxford.

MBITI, J. (1971) *New Testament Eschatology in an African Background*, Oxford.

MIDDLETON, J. and WINTER, E. H. eds (1963) *Witchcraft and Sorcery in East Africa*, London.

MIDDLETON, J. and KERSHAW, G. (1965) *The Kikuyu and Kamba of Kenya*, London.

MINER, H. ed. (1967) *The City in Modern Africa*, London.

MORGAN, W. T. W. (1967) *Nairobi City and Region*, London.

OKOT P'BITEK (1971) *The Religion of the Central Luo*, Nairobi.

OLIVER, R. and FAGE, J. D. (1962) *A Short History of Africa*, Harmondsworth.

OLIVER, R. and MATHEW, G. eds (1963) *History of East Africa*, vol. I, Oxford.

ORAM, N. (1965) *Towns in Africa*, London.

The Oxford Atlas for East Africa, Nairobi/London (1966).

PARKIN, D. (1969) *Neighbours and Nationals in an African City Ward*, London.

RANGER, T. O. and KIMAMBO, I. N. eds (1972) *The Historical Study of African Religion*, London.

RIGBY, P. (1969) *Cattle and Kinship Among the Gogo*, Ithaca and London.

ROBERTS, A. ed. (1968) *Tanzania Before 1900*, Nairobi.

ROSCOE, J. (1965) *The Baganda*, London (2nd ed.).

SELIGMAN, C. G. (1930) *The Races of Africa*, Oxford.

SHORTER, A. (1970) 'The Migawo—peripheral spirit possession and Christian prejudice', *Anthropos*, 65, pp. 110–26.

SHORTER, A. (1972) *Chiefship in Western Tanzania*, Oxford.

SMITH, M. G. (1956) 'On segmentary lineage systems', *Journal of the Royal Anthropological Institute*, 86, ii, pp. 39–80.

SOUTHALL, A. (1953) *Alur Society*, Cambridge.

SOUTHALL A. and GUTKIND, P. J. (1957) *Townsmen in the Making*, Kampala.

TREVOR, J. C. (1953) *Race Crossing in Man*, Cambridge.

TRIMINGHAM, J. S. (1962) *Islam in East Africa*, London.

TURNER, H. W. (1967) 'A typology for African religious movements', *Journal of Religion in Africa*, vol. I, no. 1, pp. 1–34.

TURNER, V. (1968) *The Drums of Affliction*, Oxford.

TURNER, V. (1969) *The Ritual Process*, London.

WELBOURN, F. B. and OGOT, A. (1966) *A Place to Feel at Home*, Oxford.

WILSON, M. (1959) *The Communal Rituals of the Nyakyusa*, Oxford.

Index

Abushiri, 25
Acholi tribe, 23
Adolescence, 16, 116
African Inland Church/Mission, 88, 120
Age-sets, 32–3, 34, 35, 119
Agriculture, 11, 12, 13, 17, 22, 30, 32, 34, 35, 36, 50, 57–65, 87, 113, 118–24, 125, 127, 128, 131
Ahmaddiya Muslim Sect, 89
Akan peoples of Ghana, 40
Alur tribe, 23, 42, 97, 98
Amba tribe, 103, 105
America, Americans, 88, 115
Amin, Gen. Idi, 28, 29
Ancestor veneration, 87
Anglicans, 25, 87, 89, 90, 92, 100, 101, 111, 120
Animals, 12, 44, 46
Ankole, kingdom, 45, 97
Arabs, 15, 16, 24, 25, 39, 48, 115
Archaeology, 20, 22
Arusha Declaration, 26
Arusha tribe, 35
Asians, 15, 16, 28, 114, 115, 116, 127
Athi River, 118, 119, 120, 121, 122

Bagamoyo town, 49
Baker, Sir Samuel, 25
Balokole revivalist movement, 98
Bangladesh, 15, 16
Bantu languages, -speaking peoples, 19, 20, 21, 22, 23, 30, 40, 85

Baptists, 120
Barrett, D. B., 93
Baumann, O., 19
Beattie, J. H. M., 94
Beer-clubs, 130
Beidelman, T. O., 103, 106
Belgians, 26
Bemba tribe, 108
Birth-rate, 16
Birth-rites, 76
Bleek, W. H. I., 21
Bride-service, 68, 70
Bridewealth, 32, 34, 36, 69, 70
Britain, 3, 15, 16, 21, 25, 27, 28
British, 4, 15, 16, 24, 28, 39, 80, 89, 115, 126
Bungu tribe, *see* Ubungu chiefdom
Bunyoro-Kitara kingdom, 23, 45, 46, 97; *see also* Nyoro tribe
Burton, Sir R. F., 25
Bush-schools, 78
Bushman-Hottentot (Khoisan) peoples, 19, 20

Cameron, V. L., 25
Catechists, 78, 91
Cement factory, 122
Chagga tribe, 16, 46, 77, 86 90
Chahuta movement, 108
Chiefs (chieftains), 8, 33, 39–47
Chikanga, witch-cleanser, 109
Chinese, 27
Chope tribe, 23

150

Chunya Area (District), 125, 126, 127, 132
Church of God, 88
Churches, 8, 72, 73, 74, 78, 80, 84, 105
Chwezi (Swezi) spirits, 23, 45–6, 97, 99, 100
Clans, 36, 77, 85, 119
Clergy, 73, 91
Climate, 10, 11
Communities of affliction, 8, 94–101
Compounds, 60, 112
Congregationalists, 88
Congruence of values, 5
Conus-shell disc-emblems, 46
Co-operatives, 64
Cory, H., 99
Crime, 37, 56
Crops, 11, 12, 58, 60, 62, 119, 124, 126, 128, 130
Cross-cousin marriage, 68, 69
Cumulative opposition, 43
Cushitic languages, peoples, 21

Dar-es-Salaam city, 14, 16, 49, 51, 52, 53, 54
Democratic Party of Uganda, 28
Detribalization, 2, 4
Diop, Sheikh Anta, 18
Divination, 8, 53, 103, 105
Divine kingship, 40, 41
Divorce, 69, 71, 72, 73, 80
Dodoma town, 49
Douglas, M., 67, 94, 105
Drama, 96
Drums, 46

East African Community, 14
Education, 5, 57, 59–60, 70, 75–83, 92; see also Schools
Egypt, 40
Elopement, 74
Embu tribe, 118
Estates, plantations, 60
Ethiopians, 19
Eurasians, 19
Europeans, 15, 16, 18, 24, 25, 120, 127
Evans-Pritchard, Sir E. E. Y., 41
Exogamy, 68

Fage, J. D., 40
Family, 54, 57, 66–74, 84
Fishing, 13
Fortes, M., 41
Frazer, Sir J. G., 40

Gaba village, 110
Galla (Kenya) tribe, 21, 48, 89, 118
Galla (Tanzania) tribe, 42
Ganda tribe, kingdom of Buganda, 16, 23, 28, 39, 45, 47, 51, 77, 89–90, 110–17
Gedi ruins, 48
Geology, 10
Germans, Germany, 4, 21, 25, 26, 44, 45, 126
Ghost-marriage, 69
Gichuru, J., 27
Giriyama tribe, 27, 119
Gisu tribe, 52, 78, 103, 104, 105
God, idea of, 85–6
Gogo tribe, 16, 36, 86, 87
Gold mining, 126–7
Grant, J. A., 25
Gray, R. F. ,99, 106
Great Rift Valley, 10
Greenberg, J. H., 21
Gulliver, P. H., 7
Guruka tribe, 126, 127
Gusii tribe, 103
Guthrie, M., 21

Ha tribe, 16, 46, 97
Hadza tribe, 20
Hamites, 18, 19, 21, 30
Harambee projects, 58, 64, 123
Haya tribe, 16, 90, 114
Hehe tribe, 16, 26, 44
Hima caste, 45
Hinda states, 45, 46
Honey collecting, 13, 31, 125, 130
Hospitals, 111
Housing estates, 112–13
Hunting, 13, 22, 78, 86, 105–6, 120, 125
Hydro-electric power, 13, 110, 122

Ikutha mission, 120
Imperials British East Africa Co, 25

Incorporation, principle of, 1, 6, 7, 17
Independence, 15, 26, 27, 36, 49
Independent churches, 8, 26, 84, 92, 93, 100, 114
India, 15, 16
Indirect rule, 126
Industry, 13, 49
Initiation, life-crisis and puberty rites, 32, 33, 68, 77–8, 80, 91, 94
Iramba tribe, 86
Iraqw (Mbulu) tribe, 21
Iringa town, 109
Iru caste, 45
Islam, 8, 15, 28, 39, 46, 48, 78, 84, 88–9, 92, 98–9, 111
Issanzu tribe, 86
Itenda chiefdom, 106
Ivory, 24, 25, 44, 45, 68, 120

Jie tribe, 32, 34, 35,
Jinja town, 49
Joking partners, 69–70

Kabaka Mutesa I, 89
Kabaka Mutesa II, 28
Kabaka Mwanga, 89
Kaguru tribe, 103, 105, 106
Kakungulu, Prince, 28
Kalenjin peoples, 4, 22, 25
Kamba tribe, 98, 118–24
Kampala city, 14, 16, 49, 50, 51, 52, 53, 55, 110–17
Karimojong tribe, 32, 34, 35, 36, 86
Kasese railway terminus, 110
Kayoya, M., 32
Kenya African National Union (KANU), 27
Kenya African Union (KAU), 27
Kenya Army, 121
Kenya Meat Corporation, 122
Kenya People's Union (KPU), 27
Kenyatta, Jomo, 27
Kibwezi settlement, 120, 124
Kigezi District, 114
Kikuyu tribe 7, 15, 27, 90, 118, 120
Kilanga I, chief of Ubungu, 43
Kilwa town, 48

Kimbu tribe, 42, 43, 46, 78, 86, 97, 100, 103, 104, 105, 106, 107, 108, 125–32
King's African Rifles, 121
Kipembawe village, 127, 128
Kisenselia, Chief, 106
Kisumu town, 15
Kitunda District, 126
Kivoi, the Kamba trader, 120
Kiwanuka, B., 28, 29
Kiyui town, 118, 119, 120, 121
Konongo tribe, 42
Krapf, J. L., 120
Kuria tribe, 86, 120

Lakes, 10, 11, 12, 15, 20, 22, 23, 24, 25, 40, 41, 45, 47, 78, 110, 125
Lamu town, 48
Language, 18, 19, 20, 21, 22
League of Nations, 26
Leakey, L. S. B., 20
Lenshina, Alice, 108
Leslie, J. A. K., 54
Lettow-Vorbeck, P. von, 26
Levirate, 69
Libya, 115
Liminal ritual, 94
Livingstone, D., 25
Long-distance porterage, 44
Lucas, Bishop V., 91
Lugbara tribe, 98, 103, 106
Lule, F., 53
Lumpa Church, 108
Luo tribe, 15, 23, 27, 28, 90, 113–14, 120
Lupa gold mines and Controlled Area, 126–7
Lutherans, 88, 120
Luyia (Abaluyia) peoples, 4, 15, 114
Lwoo peoples, 23

Machakos town, 118, 120, 121, 123, 124
Maji Maji rebellion, 25, 92, 93, 108
Makindu settlement, 124
Makonde tribe, 16

Makueni re-settlement scheme, 123, 124
Malindi town, 48, 49
Marriage, 32, 51, 61, 66–74, 80
Masai tribe, 23, 30, 31, 33, 35, 36, 90, 118
Masasi diocese, 91
Masinde, E., 93
Matriliny, 40, 41, 67–8, 70
Matwiga village settlement, 128, 129, 130, 131, 132
Mau Mau campaign, 27, 93
Maulidi gatherings, 92
Mazimbo village, 128, 129, 130, 131
Mbale town, 49
Mbeveta, Chief, 106
Mbeya Town, Region and Area, 125, 126, 127
Mbiti, J. S., 120
Mboya, Tom, 27, 28
Mbugwe tribe, 86, 103, 106
Mchape movement, 108
Mengo urban area, 48, 111
Merere, Chief, 43
Meru tribe, 118
Methodists, 88
Meyerowicz, E. L., 40
Middleton, J., 106
Migawo society, 46
Minerals, 13
Mining, 13
Mirambo, Chief, 25, 45
Missionaries, 25, 59, 70, 72, 73, 78, 79, 87
Mkwawa, Chief, 26, 44
Mogadishu town, 24
Mohammed, Prophet, 92
Mombasa town, 15, 48, 49, 110, 120, 122
Moravians, 88, 90, 129
Mountains, 10, 23, 35, 77, 87, 110, 118
Mozambique, 24
Mtito Ndei settlement, 124
Mulango mission, 120
Multi-variate distances, 19, 22
Munyigumba, Chief, 44
Mwambani village, 127
Mwanza town, 49

Nairobi city, 14, 15, 49, 50, 51, 55, 110, 120
Nakuru town, 49
Nandi tribe, 32–3, 35, 38, 90, 103
Ndorobo tribe (Asi), 31, 33
Negriforms, 20
Negrilloes, 20
Negroes, 18, 19, 20, 21, 22, 40
Ngala, R., 27
Ngoni tribe, 24, 43
Nigeria, 22
Nilotes, 19, 20 22, 24
Nomadism, 31–2, 34, 35
Nubians, 89
Nyakyusa tribe, 87, 106, 107, 129, 130
Nyamwezi tribe, 3, 16, 42, 43, 44, 46, 86, 97, 100, 103, 108, 126
Nyerere, Julius K., 26
Nyiha tribe, 129
Nyika tribe, 118
Nyisamba Kimbu people, 126, 127–8
Nyitumba Kimbu people, 126, 127–8
Nyoro tribe, 103, 114, 115, *see also* Bunyoro-Kitara kingdom
Nyungu-ya-Mawe, Chief, 43, 44, 45

Obote Milton A., 28, 29
Oginga Odinga, Jaramogi, 27
Olduvai gorge, 20
Oliver, R., 40
Oman, 24
Oracles, 107
Ordeals, 107–8
OXFAM, 128

Padhola tribe, 23
Pakistan, 15, 16
Pare tribe, 78, 86
Parkin, D., 51, 113
Particularism, 7, 93
Pastoralists, 7, 19, 20, 23, 30–8, 39, 41
Patriliny, 67–8, 70, 76
Peace Corps, 115
Pemba Island, 11
Pentecostalism, 100, 101
Periplus of the Erythrean Sea, 24
Peters, K., 25
Pimbwe tribe, 86

Pluralism, 1, 2, 4, 6, 7, 17, 71
Poison ordeal, 107
Polygamy, 61, 69, 71
Population, 14–15, 16, 17, 49, 50
Port Bell, 110
Portugal, 24, 48
Presbyterians, 88, 120
Prostitution, 55, 115
Pygmies, 19, 20

Quakers, 88

Races, 18, 19
Railways, 14, 25, 27, 89, 110, 111, 114, 120
Rainfall, 11, 87, 119, 125
Religion, 5, 8, 33, 41, 77, 84–93, 94, 96, 104
Re-settlement schemes, 60, 123, 125–32
Rhodesia, 130
Rigby, P. J., ix, 53
Rituals, 8, 32, 34, 41, 53, 77, 85, 87, 94, 95
Rivers, 10, 13, 21, 23, 24, 118, 125, 126
Roman Catholics, 25, 28, 87, 89, 91, 92, 98, 100, 101, 111, 120, 128, 129
Rwanda-Burundi, 24, 25, 97
Rwandese, 54, 114

Safwa tribe, 129
Sagara tribe, 23, 67
Said, Seyyid, 24
Salvation Army, 120
Sandawe tribe, 20
Sangu tribe, 43, 129
Saudi-Arabia, 115
Schools, 78–81, 116
Scott, P. C., 120
Sebei tribe, 35
Segmentary state, 42
Seligman, C. G., 18, 19, 40
Sese Islands, 110
Seventh Day Adventists, 88, 120
Shetani society, 98–9, 100
Shop-keepers, 112, 116, 117
Shungwaya area, 23
Sidama people, 21

Slaves, 24, 25, 88
Smith, M. G., 42
Sofala town, 24
Somali tribes, 21, 89
Sonjo tribe, 86
Sorcery, 102–9
South Africa, 24, 26, 49
Southall, A., 6, 42, 96, 98, 122
Spain, 24
Spartas, Reuben, 93
Speke, J. H., 25
Spirit mediums, 46, 94, 96, 103, 107, 119
Spirit possession, 8, 46, 94–101, 103
Spirits, 86–7, 95, 98
Stanley, Sir H. M., 25, 89
Stock-raising, 7, 12, 30–8, 44, 45, 87, 119, 122
Stratification, social, 6, 32
Sudan, 114
Sudanic kingdoms, languages, 22, 40
Sukuma tribe, 3, 16, 42, 46, 97, 103
Sultan Hamud settlement, 122
Sumbwa tribe, 46
Super-cities, 49–50
Super-tribes, 4
Swahili language (ki-Swahili), 25, 82, 98–9, 121
Swantz, L., 51, 52

Tabora town, 48, 109, 126
Taita hills, 23
Tanga town, 49
Tanganyika African National Union (TANU), 26, 129
Tanganyika Development Corporation, 128
Tanzania Tobacco Corporation, 130
Taturu tribe (Tatoga, Mang'ati), 22
Taveta tribe, 118
Ten-house-cell system, 106, 129
Tharaka tribe, 118
Toro tribe, 114
Tourism, 12, 13, 14
Towns, 4, 15, 16, 48–56, 57, 60
Trevor, J. C., 20
Tribalism, 2, 7, 93
Tribes, 1, 2, 3, 4, 5

Tsavo National Park, 124
Tsetse fly, 12, 17, 44, 124, 125, 126
Turkana tribe, 35
Turner, V. W., 8, 94
Tusi tribe, 24

Ubungu chiefdom, 39, 43, 126, 127, 129
Uganda Martyrs, 25, 79
Uganda People's Congress, 28
Ujamaa, 12, 26, 27, 58, 62, 63, 64, 131
United Nations Organization, 26
Universities, 81–2, 83, 111
Urban villages, 4, 52, 113, 114
Urbanization, 4, 8, 15, 48–56, 57

Vegetation, 10, 11, 12

Welbourn, F. B., 93
Wikangulu, 106
Wildlife, 12
Wilson, M., 87, 107
Witch-eradication, cleansing, 108–9
Witch-finding, 8, 53, 102–9
Woman marriage, 69
Wood carving, 120–1
World War I, 26, 120
World War II, 26, 127

Zaïre, 20, 25, 114
Zambia, 27, 108
Zanzibar Island, 11, 24, 25, 48
Zaramo tribe, 16, 51, 52, 53, 67
Ziba, see Haya tribe
Zimba tribe, 24, 48
Zulu tribe, 16